Penguin Critical Studies
Advisory Editor: Bryan Loughrey

The Poetry of Keats

Brian Stone

Penguin Books

PENGUIN BOOKS

Published by the Penguin Group
Penguin Books Ltd, 27 Wrights Lane, London W8 5TZ, England
Penguin Books USA Inc., 375 Hudson Street, New York, New York 10014, USA
Penguin Books Australia Ltd, Ringwood, Victoria, Australia
Penguin Books Canada Ltd, 10 Alcorn Avenue, Toronto, Ontario, Canada M4V 3B2
Penguin Books (NZ) Ltd, 182–190 Wairau Road, Auckland 10, New Zealand

Penguin Books Ltd, Registered Offices: Harmondsworth, Middlesex, England

First published 1992
10 9 8 7 6 5 4 3 2

Typeset by DatIX International Limited, Bungay, Suffolk
Set in 9/11 pt Monophoto Times
Printed in England by Clays Ltd, St Ives plc

Contents

Acknowledgements   vii

Foreword: The Use of This Book   ix

Keats's Life and Work: A Table of Dates   1

Introduction   4

1. From the Beginnings to *Endymion*   16
2. 1818 and *Isabella*   29
3. *Hyperion*   34
4. Dreams through Stained Glass: *The Eve of St Agnes* and *The Eve of St Mark*   44
5. Death, Love and Fame: Shorter Poems from December 1818 to April 1819   54
6. The Spring Odes of 1819   66
7. *Lamia*   90
8. *The Fall of Hyperion. A Dream*   102
9. Dramatic Attempts and the Last Shorter Poems   112
10. The Forms of Keats's Poetry   130

Select Bibliography and Abbreviations Used in the Text   148

Literary Glossary   149

Glossary of Literary Terms   155

Index of Keats's Poems   157

Acknowledgements

Miriam Allott's *The Poems of John Keats* (1970) is the source of all my quotations from Keats's poems, as well as of many of the glosses and references to sources. It is a monumental work on which I have greatly depended, and I make grateful acknowledgement to the author. The biographies of Keats by Aileen Ward and Robert Gittings have always been by me, and my quotations from the letters are from the late Robert Gittings's selection. I hope that I have made clear my debt to them, and to the authors and editors of all the books listed in the Select Bibliography and acknowledged in my text.

Kensington, February 1992

Foreword: The Use of This Book

This contribution to the Critical Studies series is a teaching book about the work of a poet who developed rapidly from immature enthusiasm for poetry to mature production of some of the loveliest and most profound poems in the English language. The line of development is consistent throughout, in language, poetic form, subject matter, meaning and view of life; so that study of the later major poetry always benefits from close knowledge of earlier works. It is therefore recommended that this book be read continuously from the beginning, and not used as a kind of critical quarry, in which selective digging may be directed from the index of poems, though of course such use is possible.

The aim is to offer the reader or student an account of Keats's development, which even in the final stages is still that of a young man. To this end, all the important poems are taken in broadly chronological order of composition, and an account of them is given: a modest critical and analytical commentary is runningly incorporated. A number of critics writing in the nineteenth and twentieth centuries, including Keats's fellow-poets, are quoted, though sparingly.

Biographical matters are mentioned in the text, but only when they are relevant to the poetry. Following this foreword is a table of the important dates in Keats's life and works.

Chapter 10 offers some account of Keats's versification and use of poetic forms, again in chronological order. Students are especially advised to read it, because so many books about poetry fail to comment on technical matters of composition. Their authors write as if problems of poetic genre, metre, stanza, rhyme and so forth are surmounted as if by magic by the poets. The truth is different, as anyone who has tried to write poetry knows. Sections in this chapter should be read in conjunction with the main consideration of particular poems treated in Chapters 1–9.

The book concludes with a select bibliography, a glossarial index which lists people mentioned in the text, including poets, then a glossary of literary terms and finally an index of Keats's poems cited in the text.

Keats's Life and Work: A Table of Dates

1795 (31 October) Born in Finsbury, London, to Thomas Keats, ostler at the Swan and Hoop Inn, and Frances Keats (née Jennings).

1797 (28 February) Brother George born.

1799 (18 November) Brother Tom born.

1801 (28 April) Brother Edward born.

1802 Edward dies.

1803 (3 June) Sister, Frances Mary (Fanny) born.

      (August) Goes to Rev. John Clarke's school in Enfield, north London.

1804 (15 April) Father dies in riding accident.

      (27 June) Mother marries William Rawlings, and the Keats children move in with their grandparents, John and Alice Jennings, in Enfield.

1805 (March) John Jennings dies. Alice and the children move back nearer London, to Edmonton.

1806 Mother leaves Rawlings.

1810 Mother returns to look after her children, but in March dies from tuberculosis, attended by Keats.

      (July) John Sandall and Richard Abbey are appointed guardians of the Keats children.

1811 Leaves school to become apprentice to Thomas Hammond, surgeon and apothecary.

      Completes translation of the *Aeneid* begun at school.

      George and Tom start work in Abbey's counting-house.

1812 Byron: *Childe Harold*, Cantos I and II.

1813 Leigh Hunt imprisoned for libelling the Prince Regent.

1814 'Imitation of Spenser' (first known poem).

      (December) Grandmother dies. Fanny Keats moves in with the Abbeys.

      Cary: blank verse translation of Dante's *Purgatorio* and *Paradiso*.

      Wordsworth: *The Excursion*.

1815 (2 February) Sonnet on Hunt's release from prison.

      (October) Enters Guy's Hospital as a student.

1816   (May) Sonnet 'O Solitude' published in Hunt's *Examiner*.

(July) Qualifies as apothecary.

(October) 'On First Looking into Chapman's Homer'.

Meets Hunt, Benjamin Haydon, John Hamilton Reynolds, Joseph Severn.

(December) 'Sleep and Poetry'.

Tells guardian he will be a poet, not an apothecary.

Shelley: *Alastor*.

Hunt: *The Story of Rimini*.

Coleridge: *Christabel* and 'Kubla Khan'.

1817   (February) Hunt shows Keats's poems to Shelley, Godwin and Hazlitt.

(March) Moves to Hampstead with George and Tom.

First sees Elgin Marbles with Haydon and Reynolds.

Poems published by C. & J. Ollier.

(April–November) Leaves London to work on *Endymion*, staying in Margate, Canterbury and lastly in Oxford with Bailey.

(May) Meets Isabella Jones.

Meets Charles Armitage Brown and Richard Woodhouse.

(December) Meets Wordsworth.

Ideas on poetry expressed in letters: 'the holiness of the Heart's affections and the truth of the Imagination', 'intensity', 'negative capability', etc.

1818   (January–February) Hears Hazlitt's lectures on the English poets.

(March–April) Nurses Tom in Teignmouth, where he writes *Isabella*.

(April) *Endymion* published by Taylor & Hessey.

(May) Brother George marries Georgiana Wylie and (June) leaves for America.

Ideas on poetry expressed in letters – (27 February) to Taylor, (3 May) Reynolds, (27 October) Woodhouse.

(June–August) Tours the Lakes and Scotland with Brown; only book taken, Cary's Dante.

(mid August) Sore throat forces Keats's return to London, where he nurses Tom till his death on 1 December. Working on *Hyperion*.

(September) Meets Fanny Brawne.

Hostile criticism of *Endymion* in *Blackwood's*, the *Quarterly Review* and the *British Critic*.

(December) Moves in with Brown at Wentworth Place, Hampstead (now Keats House), after Tom's death.

1819   (January) In Chichester with Brown. *The Eve of St Agnes*.

(February) *The Eve of St Mark*.

(March) Abandons *Hyperion*.

(April) 'As Hermes once', 'La Belle Dame Sans Merci'.

(April–May) The five Spring Odes: 'Ode to Psyche', 'Ode to a Nightingale', 'Ode on a Grecian Urn', 'Ode on Melancholy', 'Ode on Indolence'.

(May) George writes from America about his money troubles. Keats tries without success to get some of his inheritance from Abbey.

(June) In love with Fanny Brawne, but leaves London in order to be free to compose poetry.

(June–October) First in Portsmouth, then in Winchester, composes *Lamia*, *Otho the Great* (with Brown), *King Stephen*, *The Fall of Hyperion. A Dream*, 'To Autumn', *The Cap and Bells*.

(December) Abandons *The Fall of Hyperion* as too Miltonic.

Becomes engaged to Fanny Brawne.

Increasingly unwell.

Byron: *Don Juan*, Cantos I and II published anonymously by John Murray.

1820   (January) George in London to try to raise money, with little success, and leaves again for America.

(3 February) Has severe lung haemorrhage and is never well again.

(May–June) Alone in Kentish Town (north London) and after second lung haemorrhage moves in with Hunt and family.

(July) *Lamia, Isabella, The Eve of St Agnes and Other Poems* published in the volume generally known as 'Poems 1820'.

(August) Nursed by Fanny and Mrs Brawne. Shelley invites him to Italy.

Byron: *Don Juan*, Cantos III and IV published.

(September) Leaves for Italy in the care of Severn.

(21 October) Arrives in Naples, held in quarantine for ten days.

(November) Goes to Rome.

1821   (23 February) Dies and is buried in the Protestant Cemetery in Rome.

Introduction

In the history of English poetry, John Keats, in his poetry, his letters and his personal life, is phenomenal in a special way. Voluminous contemporary material, written by himself, his many friends and supporters, fellow-poets and critics, has been reinforced by continuous critical and biographical attention over the century and three quarters since his death in 1821, so that he is one of the most well studied of poets. Among readers of poetry, his reputation grew steadily in the nineteenth century, after a poor start, and today, on the basis of only a few poems, including especially the odes and the letters, he is probably rated more highly than ever. The poetic immortality he so ardently desired is certainly his. This short study is of Keats's poetry, not of his life or his letters, both of which are referred to only when it is considered necessary in discussion of the poetry. The phenomenon to be considered here is thus the poetic output, over little more than four years, 1816 to 1819, of a young man who started by surging into the writing of poetry with a blazing and often embarrassing enthusiasm, developed through ruthless self-criticism and hard experience of life into a Romantic poet of original lyrical and narrative capability, and was just beginning to cap that with a profound maturity and an acceptance of a tragic vision of life, when tuberculosis weakened his poetic and spiritual life, and then killed him.

The society in which Keats grew up was one of the rising middle class in London, which was going through volatile and changeable times. England was in the aftermath of Waterloo (1815) and going through the dynamic processes of the Industrial Revolution, which brought huge changes in the way people lived and worked, together with a rapidly expanding population. Towns and cities became forcing houses for new social and economic processes, the operation of which could, and did, aggravate poverty and spread prosperity. Political life and activity reflected the often violent tension between victorious reaction following the defeat of Napoleonic France, and struggling liberalism of the English democratic kind, which had been strongly stimulated by two great historic events in which ideas of liberty and equality achieved initial triumph and then remained potent in Europe – the American War of Independence (1776–83) and the French Revolution (1789).

The Keats family became prosperous through what we should now call hotel management: Keats's father was head ostler at the Swan and Hoop Inn, and when he died in a riding accident, Keats being eight at the time, he left his family fairly well off. Subsequent developments in the family, together with the mean maladministration of the Keats children's hereditary entitlements by their guardian, explain the constant references to shortage of money in the letters. But at the time when the education of the Keats children was being considered, money was available for the kind of education desired.

It appears that some thought was given to sending Keats to Harrow, but eventually Clarke's School, a liberal establishment catering for about seventy or eighty boys, was chosen. Like the academies which at adult level provided Dissenters with a scholarly higher education which rivalled, and in some respects excelled, that of the regular universities of Oxford and Cambridge, it was a progressive place, combining humane social organization and a wide-ranging curriculum. Individuality was allowed to flourish, in contrast to the practice in established educational institutions, where conformism was encouraged. Here, particularly through his friendship with Charles Cowden Clarke, the headmaster's son, was laid the foundation for Keats's entry into the liberal intellectual life of London, with its keen activity in all the arts and its idealistic libertarian stance in politics.

At Clarke's School, Keats's lifelong enthusiasm for music, the visual arts and literature was established. His repeatedly expressed love of Mozart derived from such things as attending Mozart concerts at an inn in the city, and listening to Charles Cowden Clarke's playing of the piano. His love of painting and sculpture came from looking at books of engravings – this was before the age of good printed colour reproduction – and visiting public museums and private art galleries. But nourishment of what was to become his specialization came from the wide field of literature which was organically encompassed by study of modern languages, classical Latin and English literature. The process of education in these included practice in paraphrase and translation, and it was in this way that Keats came by his extraordinary knowledge of, and feeling for, English poetry and drama and the classical heritage. It is known that Keats translated the whole of Virgil's *Aeneid*, some of it while still at school, and the rest soon after leaving and becoming apprentice to the surgeon and apothecary Thomas Hammond. All the arts mentioned above figure overtly in his early poetry and are subtly subsumed into his mature work, in original transformation.

Keats's use of classical mythology in three major narrative poems,

Endymion, *Hyperion*, and *The Fall of Hyperion. A Dream*, and a number of lyrics, including 'Ode to Psyche' and 'Ode on a Grecian Urn', may prove a stumbling-block to students no longer reared on the classics – or indeed the Bible. So I have tried whenever possible to explain the myths and Keats's use of them while treating the poetry, rather than to include a selective classical dictionary as an appendix. This should work to some extent in the odes and the Hyperion poems, but when studying *Endymion*, in which Keats's enthusiasm for the classics is most profusely expressed, students should have a classical dictionary or companion as a stand-by. The reason is that he often mentions a name in passing, as if he expects the reader to know the relevant myth and to savour its poetic force. One example of the very many is Orion, who is briefly adduced for atmospheric purposes in Book II, line 198, to illustrate the yearning of Endymion for his moon goddess, Cynthia. Endymion is described as like 'blind Orion hungry for the morn'. To savour the reference, one needs to know who Orion was. The dictionary tells us that he was a giant who was made drunk, and then blinded while asleep, by a king who wanted to avoid keeping his promise to give Orion his daughter in marriage. When he awoke and found that he was blind, the giant had himself conducted 'to a place where the rising sun was seen with greatest advantage. Here he turned his face towards the luminary, and, as it is reported, he immediately recovered his eyesight, and hastened to punish the perfidious cruelty of Oenipion' (Lemprière, 428b).

After *Endymion*, classical personages and myths generally appear in the poetry with their attributes described, and sometimes adjusted, according to the specific purposes of Keats. Yet for the serious student, the dictionaries remain important to the end, as may be demonstrated by a single reference to the 'Ode on a Grecian Urn': in the fourth stanza, which describes a solemn sacrifice before a congregation whose attendance has emptied the nearby town, Keats experts have detected not only a reference to a painting by Claude and 'a detail incorporated from the Elgin Marbles' (Allott, 536), but also the source in John Lemprière's *Classical Dictionary* (1788) for the ruling idea of the whole stanza. This is drawn from the story of the handsome young Hyacinthus, who was loved by Apollo, and also by Zephyrus, the god of the west wind. When Apollo and Hyacinthus were playing at quoits, Zephyrus in jealousy blew the quoit at the head of the youth, killing him. The beautiful festival celebrating those events is depicted by Keats, and the poetic meaning of his conclusion to the stanza is built upon Lemprière's last words in the entry on 'Hyacinthia': 'During the latter part of the festivity, all were eager to be present at the games, and the city was left almost without inhabitants' (Lemprière, 288a). Charles Cowden Clarke reported that Keats learned by heart passages of Lemprière, which provided his main but not only classical inspiration. Traces of information from John Potter's *Antiquities of Greece* (1697) also figure in the poetry.

No less illuminating than Keats's absorption of the myths and spirit of the classical world is his induction into the world of contemporary politics, and his constancy in maintaining within it the views he developed from the outset. But there is a difference in the way his political outlook is reflected in his poetry. While the representation of classical mythology is always overt, even when he places new emphasis on people and events, there is very little direct representation of his political opinions in his poetry. His furious delineation of the murderous brothers of Isabella as grasping capitalists has no parallels in his major poetry. In minor poems he does directly denounce political events of which he disapproves, and celebrate events of which he approves. Such are the youthful anti-royalist outburst against the celebration of the anniversary of the restoration of Charles II, and the attack on the 'wretched crew' who imprisoned Leigh Hunt for libelling the Prince Regent. Such, too, is the opening of Book III of *Endymion*, in which Keats castigates royalty and the Established Church at some length.

But there is no major poem in which Keats presents a detailed working out of progressive ideas, such as Blake composed throughout his life, or Wordsworth offered in his early years, or Shelley constantly wrote. Instead, there are two aspects of his work which contribute to such an end, both of which show Keats more as a moral and social idealist than a bred-in-the-bone politician who desires to make an orderly and practical whole of his political ideas and feelings. One of these is in the letters, where he repeatedly expresses detestation of tyranny and sympathy with social and personal suffering. Reading the letters, one is never in doubt about what I have called his moral and social idealism. The other aspect lies in the whole thrust of several of his major poems, particularly those which he builds upon a mythological basis – *Endymion*, *Hyperion* and *The Fall of Hyperion. A Dream*. In the latter two poems especially, the idea of one dispensation of gods being replaced by a better one is absolutely constant, and that stance constitutes an idealistic hope which is applied to the whole universe and all the activities in it. It is a political stance, but, more than that, it is an aesthetic one, and the two strands of thought are fused in a single line which will be quoted again in this study. It is the hope, even the expectation – for on this subject Keats is optimistic from the beginning –

> That first in beauty should be first in might;
> (*Hyperion*, II, 229)

That aesthetic strand – pursuit by practice and advocacy of the better-ment of poetry by ever more intense observation and delineation of beauty in life, the method being the exercise of what he called 'the true voice of feeling' (*Letters*, 292) – is woven through the poetry as constantly as the political one is woven through the prose. It is therefore usual, even if it appears simplistic, to phrase the assertion in this way: that in Keats, aesthetics and politics are indivisible. He is always concerned with what he called 'Liberty's Emblazoning', which is a matter of both practical politics and poetic practice.

In discussing the work of such a poet as Keats, the word 'Romantic' has become indispensable, but it should not be used loosely, that is, without some knowledge of its historic meaning in discussion of early nineteenth-century literature. The latter is the product of a cultural movement involving a profound shift in sensibility in Europe and North America, which is usually regarded as having been sparked off by the French Revolution. 'Romanticism' embraced not only literature but all the arts, and all systems of thought which related to the conduct of individual and social life, in which politics, religion and morals were probably the most important.

Butler, in her introduction to *Romantics, Rebels and Reactionaries*, rightly warns, 'Twentieth-century thinking about early nineteenth-century literature is cramped by a single formidable word: Romantic' (1). One view is that Romanticism can be understood as 'a violent reaction to the Enlightenment' (*Oxford Companion to Literature*, 1985, 842b). But Butler regards it as simplistic 'to see late eighteenth-century Western society as a serene and static world, rudely galvanized by the storming of the Bastille in 1789'. She encourages the taking of a wider historical view, which sees elements of Romanticism as developing from seeds existing in the period of the Enlightenment, that is, the eighteenth century. And she observes of the word 'Romantic' that 'the poets concerned would not have used it of themselves. Not until the 1860s did "the Romantics" become an accepted collective name for Blake, Wordsworth, Coleridge, Scott, Byron, Shelley and Keats.'

That said, some preliminary idea of Romanticism as applied to English poetry, based largely on the *Oxford Companion*, may be given, as it will help in the study of Keats. The period of Romanticism was between 1770 and 1848. Its 'profound shift in sensibility' was expressed politically in sympathy with 'the revolutions in America and France and popular wars of independence in Poland, Spain, Greece, and elsewhere. Emotionally it expressed an extreme assertion of the self and the value of individual experience ... socially it championed progressive causes ... The stylistic keynote of Romanticism is intensity, and its watchword is "Imagination".' All that may be contrasted with the generalizing tendency of eighteenth-century principles, which are expressed very simply in Pope's dictum:

> True wit is nature to advantage dress'd,
> What oft was thought, but ne'er so well express'd.
> ('An Essay on Criticism', 297–8)

In the development of Romanticism, the non-classical past, in the rediscovery of medieval literature in English, Scots English and Celtic, exerted an influence. So too did the work of German writers, especially Goethe and Schiller, together with such philosophic critics as A. W. von Schlegel, who affected the way British writers wrote and thought.

In subject matter the Romantic poets 'had a new intuition for the primal power of the wild landscape' and 'the spiritual correspondence between Man and Nature' (*Oxford Companion*). The conclusion of the arresting entry stresses the rebelliousness which is regarded as a characteristic of the Romantic poet, and applies with some truth to Keats: 'Romanticism expressed an unending revolt against classical form, conservative morality, authoritarian government, personal insincerity, and human moderation.'

The 'Romantic' Keats's 'unending revolt' was also against institutionalized Christianity, as several of the poems discussed here indicate. He was opposed to the Church not just on account of the moral and spiritual authority it claimed: it was also the view of life inherent in organized teaching and worship against which he rebelled. He hated such concepts as the duty of self-denial and the doctrines concerning sin and atonement, with their emphasis on guilt. Besides this, to define a major matter in simple terms, it seemed to Keats that the Church overemphasized the notion that earthly life offers a vale of tears which has to be gone through in suffering in order that the saved soul may earn and enjoy a blissful hereafter.

Keats's opposition to such life-denying ideas was radical, as his wounding reference to 'the pious frauds of religion' (*Letters*, 230) indicates. He saw intense life, as he wished both to live it and to perceive it, in reality as well as in art, threatened by Christian teaching. The here and now, with its lures of experience to be had and to be contemplated through intense imagination, was always of passionate concern to Keats in his two capacities, as a liver of life and a maker of poetry out of that life. So his attitude to life is essentially pagan, in that he often treats emotion and experience, and especially experience of love, in language and imagery drawn from religious vocabularies. His attitude is not so much an irreligious one as an attitude which transmutes the religious impulse into the artistic sphere, a sphere in which intensity of feeling and utter frankness not only suggest the highest values, but also conduce to the highest art – which in Keats's case was the form of poetry.

During Keats's lifetime, his poetry was published in three books. His first book, *Poems*, was published in 1817 by the brothers Ollier, who were as alarmed as Keats's friends by its poor sales and the absence of critical notice. Charles Cowden Clarke noted that '"the book might have emerged in Timbuctoo" for all the interest that it aroused' (Gittings, 179). It contained thirty-three poems, including three verse epistles to friends and fourteen sonnets: but the most interesting were the two longish poems, 'I stood tip-toe upon a little hill', which was placed second, and *Sleep and Poetry*, which concluded the youthful collection. Only thirteen months later, in April 1818, Keats's longest poem, *Endymion*, was published by Taylor & Hessey, who also published his third book, *Lamia, Isabella, The Eve of St Agnes and Other Poems* in 1820.

Endymion brought a storm of harsh criticism from traditional literary publications such as *Blackwood's*, the *Quarterly* and the *British Critic*. It was harsh because the critics not only poured scorn on the poetry, but also attacked Keats for writing poetry at all; the thrust of their criticism was therefore political as well as aesthetic. Here was a lower middle-class man, they complained, who had not even been to university, presuming to base a 'poetic romance' on classical mythology, which he presented in an obscure style, while demonstrating excessive interest in sexual relationships and apparently trying to establish a new poetic order to supplant traditional practice. Such a man, they urged, should go back to the trade of apothecary for which he had been trained. The fact that some of the things these critics wrote have been approved by modern scholars, who are as wary of apprentice work as their forebears, has received less attention than a myth that grew up in Keats's lifetime. This was that his spirit was virtually destroyed by the hostile reception of *Endymion*, and that consequently he soon after went into a decline which proved fatal. This myth was believed by Byron and Shelley, both of whom were already permanently living in Italy. Despite his sympathy, Byron is remembered in this connection for the aristocratic disdain in his *Don Juan*, which he expressed in the searing couplet, with its demeaning triple rhyme,

> 'Tis strange the mind, that very fiery particle,
> Should let itself be snuff'd out by an article.
>
> (XI, lx)

Shelley, on the other hand, used his aberrant belief to fuel the magnificent elegy on the death of Keats, *Adonais*.

Unfortunately for those two noble poets, and the sentimental Victorian tradition whose adherents were content to believe the myth, the truth was different. Keats was a sterner critic of himself than any other, and he shrugged off the political slurs on himself and his class. While he remained well, his determination to become a major English poet was stronger than anything else in his life, including his love for Fanny Brawne. The result was the 1820 volume, which contained most of the poems for which Keats is still renowned, with one or two important exceptions such as *The Fall of Hyperion. A Dream* and the 'Ode on Indolence'.

Keats's sturdy will to shape his own poetic art and destiny is demonstrated at almost every stage of his career. Staunch friends of his youth such as Leigh Hunt and John Hamilton Reynolds, and Charles Armitage Brown later, were gently pushed away from his poetry because he came to see that their impact on his work was not beneficial. Even as early as the writing of *Endymion*, Keats deliberately restricted the access to his work of the brilliantly intellectual Shelley, to whom, when virtually on the way to the grave, he offered gratuitous advice on poetic composition. He ardently defended his texts in discussion with his publisher Taylor, and with Woodhouse, the firm's lawyer and practical devotee of his work; since they, as the people responsible for marketing his poetry, held the whip hand, Keats sometimes had to give way, and the account of their negotiations over matters of poetic taste, as well as of textual adjustments, illuminates his determination to be his own kind of poet.

Keats seems to me almost always to be writing with elder poets looking over his shoulder; to be conscious that they are there to help him, but to be aware that there is danger in accepting their help, if he is to express his own poetic vision. Shakespeare seems constantly to be there, and to be so in harmony with his vision, and the language in which he wishes to present it, that there is neither conflict nor tension. He can breathe down Keats's neck without harm to the younger poet's originality. But with all the other poets whom he studied at different times, with the possible exception of Dante, his admiration was often accompanied uneasily by a feeling of being threatened. It was less obviously so with Spenser, because his influence on Keats in prosody, medievalism and allegory belongs to the first half of Keats's poetic life, and was gently shed as Keats moved into the next stage of his development.

This was at a time when the poetry of his two elder contemporaries, Wordsworth and Coleridge, came seriously to his notice; both, but Wordsworth especially, acknowledged the powerful influence of Milton. And it was Milton, with his elevated epic subject, his stately language in original constructions – original in English, that is, because some of them derived from Latin – and his flexible and ornate use of blank verse as a narrative form, who drove Keats to the task of emulation. Of course he did not wish to copy Milton, but in writing first *Hyperion* and then *The Fall of Hyperion. A Dream*, he set out to describe the kind of Fall which is the subject of *Paradise Lost*, but only as a prelude to an ensuing and directly consequent triumph of progress. In each poem he expended his main creative effort on the Fall, in this case of the Titans, who had to be got rid of so that the more beautiful Olympians might take over. Then, looking at what he had written, he felt that he had been diverted from expressing his real self by the influence of Milton's language. The most conclusive of several statements about it is made to his brother George in September 1819: 'The Paradise lost though so fine in itself is a corruption of our Language – it should be kept as it is unique – a curiosity . . . I have but lately stood on my guard against Milton. Life to him would be death to me' (*Letters*, 325). And to Reynolds at the same time, he explained that he had given up *The Fall of Hyperion. A Dream* because 'there were too many Miltonic inversions in it'.

Of Dryden and Dante in Keats, a little must be said. It was Dryden's narrative art, in poems written in heroic couplets, that in 1819 attracted Keats, who was constant in his conviction that the summit of poetic art could best be reached by writing long narrative poems. That contrasts with the taste of today, which tends to concentrate on lyrics: Keats would probably have been surprised to learn that his odes are regarded as his best work, and he died believing that though he would be among the English poets at his death, his failure to complete a major long poem would tell against him. It was not just the Neo-Classical prosody of Dryden's art that attracted Keats. Other factors were Dryden's large humanity, which allowed him to range free of Neo-Classical preoccupations with honour and its related pathos, his psychological realism and his linguistic economy. The result in Keats's work was *Lamia*. The influence of Dante shows in Keats's treatment of subject, and in two poems especially: the sonnet 'As Hermes once took to his feathers light' and *The Fall of Hyperion. A Dream*. The Dantean element in Keats can best be defined as a power to spiritualize the subject by presenting it in visionary terms. The poem becomes a quest for perfection through the fulfilment of a vision, and that vision is the purer and more desirable on account of the elements of baser life which oppose it. That is true of both the poems cited.

Only two of Keats's contemporaries seriously influenced him: Wordsworth and Hazlitt. The former's achievement in writing long philosophical poems, such as *The Excursion*, seemed to him worth emulating, though he was suspicious of the autobiographical and philosophical elements in them. In considering Milton and Wordsworth together, Keats thought that Wordsworth had the greater humanity, but he distinguished in him a quality that he called 'the egotistical sublime', which he hoped to avoid himself. He preferred that a poet's life and beliefs should be expressed, if at all, indirectly. His works should be the means by which he impressed the world: hence his profound assertion in a letter to the George Keatses early in 1819: 'Shakespeare led a life of Allegory: his works are the comment on it' (*Letters*, 218).

Like most of the statements dashed off in the communicative urgency of letter-writing, that is an illuminating idea which is not the product of a chain of reasoning; it is rather the shaped effusion of a mind which shows its true understanding of life and art without logical or philosophical discipline to control it. And the absence of that control was especially valued by Keats, who in a number of well-known passages in the letters asserts his trust in feelings and imagination. 'O for a Life of sensations rather than of Thoughts,' he exclaims to Bailey in November 1817 (*Letters*, 37). In the same letter he doubts whether 'anything can be known for truth by consequitive [*sic*] reasoning'. A little later he declares, 'The excellence of every art is its intensity' (*Letters*, 42), and in the same letter to the George Keatses are the much debated remarks about 'Negative Capability', which in my view have been overemphasized in connection with Keats's poetry. In essence, negative capability as recommended by him defends the right of poets to rest content with rich ambiguity, to be 'capable of being in uncertainties, Mysteries, doubts, without any irritable reaching after fact & reason'. Even much later, in September 1819, he can reinforce this idea: 'The only means of strengthening one's intellect is to make up one's mind about

13

nothing – to let the mind be a thoroughfare for all thoughts. Not a select party.'

His assertion about the nature of the poet as essentially disappearing into the work of art he creates is especially important. Writing to Woodhouse in October 1818, he calls a poet 'the most unpoetical of any thing in existence; because he has no Identity – he is continually . . . filling some other Body.' Many of the best-known perceptions in the letters appear in figurative language. In opposition to the contemporary religious view of earthly existence as 'a vale of tears', Keats develops his own view of the world as 'The vale of Soul-making' (*Letters*, 249), and the process by which a soul is made is represented by him as the human heart going to school. The different stages the soul passes through, in coping with experience, discovering misery and oppression, and eventually recognizing what Wordsworth called 'the burden of the mystery', are represented as chambers in a mansion. Such ideas are poetic rather than philosophic, and it seems to me a mistake to think of Keats as a philosophic poet – unless the bundle of metaphorical and abstract assertions mentioned here and in subsequent chapters in connection with the poetry may be called philosophical.

It needs to be said that, whether the system of thought and feeling defined in the letters and expressed in the poems be called philosophic or not, it is one peculiar to Keats, and it remains consistent. He found in Hazlitt, the other contemporary besides Wordsworth who seriously influenced him, many ideas about poets and poetry with which he agreed, and it was Hazlitt who helped to maintain Keats's political idealism in its pure and forceful state. Of particular interest in discussing Hazlitt and Keats is that the latter incorporated Hazlitt's famous word 'gusto' in his definition of 'the poetical Character itself': 'It lives in gusto, be it foul or fair, high or low . . . What shocks the virtuous philosopher, delights the camelion [*sic*] Poet.' But his opposition to philosophy as a useful element in poetic composition, as expressed in *Lamia* (II, 229–38) and quoted on p. 99, does not always cloud his apprehension of what philosophy might be. In the long letter to the George Keatses of spring 1819, he states his view that the very quality which makes for good poetry, which is the instinctive response to experience or observation, whether 'erroneous' or true, might make poetry 'not so fine a thing as philosophy'. But his challenge to reason, and his advocacy of the instinct and the imagination as the crowning productive powers of the poet, remain.

The quotations from the letters in this introduction and in the body of the book following should not be taken as anything more than selective evidence of Keats's thinking about poetry. The letters are a quite separate masterpiece of literature, and they should be studied as 'the most complete portrait we have of any English poet' (*Letters*, xix) They represent the frank autobiography of a developing poet who wrote about himself and his thoughts, and sent first drafts of poems to family and friends. The letters to his young sister Fanny are full of solicitude and fun: he wrote to her from Scotland after an exhausting day: '[I am] so fatigued that when I am asleep you might sew my nose to my great toe and trundle me round the town like a Hoop without waking me.' Those to his brother George and his wife Georgiana in America run to such enormous length, with their mixture of observations both trivial and profound on people and the world about him, their off-the-cuff pronouncements about politics, religion and philosophy, and their open exposure of his emotional life, that they are generally referred to as 'journal letters'. He could record receiving a black eye from a white cricket ball, and launch at once into a discussion about how the pleasure of life can be interrupted by sudden woe, and about the 'animal eagerness' which humans share with beasts and birds. As his exuberance declines with his health, the knowledge of coming death and his despairing love for Fanny Brawne bring one of the most tragic conclusions in English literature. The *Letters* must be read.

So must the poetry, to which this book is conceived as a guide, in which narration – following a poem through from start to finish – goes hand in hand with commentary. In this introduction, a few signposts have been used as indicators: each of the chapters constitutes an introduction to a poem or group of poems. In the study of Keats sequence is essential, because any account of his poetic career should chart his steadily deepening understanding, through experience, of passionate, idealistic life and its expression in poetry. The reality of that experience, with its promises and occasional gifts of happiness, and its visitations of misery, pain and grief, provides the ground for the continuous development of his poetic power. Knowledge of *Endymion* and other early poems, and the letters of 1817, is the necessary basis upon which to build understanding and appreciation of the poetic achievements of 1819.

1. From the Beginnings to *Endymion*

Most of the sixty or so poems Keats is known to have written before *Endymion*, which was completed soon after his twenty-second birthday, were written with great facility; more than once, and usually in competition with Leigh Hunt, who initiated such literary frolics, he composed a Petrarchan sonnet, with its heavy rhyme scheme and other structural demands, in a quarter of an hour. Such poems may fairly be called youthful effusions, some of which deserve attention, either because they are markers for the imminent development of an extraordinary poet, or because they are of biographical interest. Among these are poems reflecting Keats's first delight in Spenser, and his early enthusiasm for the works of Leigh Hunt, Byron and Wordsworth.

Before long Keats was to discard Leigh Hunt on account of what he regarded as his sentimentality; the delicately Romantic poet and editor who had his prison walls papered with a trellis of roses, and was the first to publish Keats's poetry, was soon to be rejected by his young protégé in favour of such models as Milton and even Shakespeare, while the Wordsworth of *The Excursion* (published 1814) was Keats's youthful lodestar. As for Byron, it was the early verse tales of Near Eastern romantic adventure, such as *The Bride of Abydos* and *The Giaour*, that Keats praised. Later he was to complain, when his guardian read to him extracts from *Don Juan*, that he had to suffer 'Lord Byron's last flash poem' (*Letters*, 311). This hostility he maintained until the end, when, reading *Don Juan* aloud with Severn on the sea voyage to Italy, he 'soon grew annoyed with Byron's unflagging cynicism and tossed the book aside' (Ward, 379).

But Spenser, whose impact on Keats was to determine the subject matter of a few of these early poems, such as 'Calidore', continued to be a useful influence, at least until the writing of *The Eve of St Agnes*, and Wordsworth remained the contemporary poet he most admired. Significant among these virtually testimonial poems, which are mainly sonnets, is 'Great spirits now on earth are sojourning' (November 1816), which celebrates Wordsworth, Leigh Hunt and Benjamin Haydon, the painter who introduced Keats to the Elgin Marbles in 1817.

The general impression given by the poems leading up to *Endymion* is of a certain range of youthful conventionality. His rejoicing at Leigh Hunt's release from imprisonment for libelling the Prince Regent – he had called the Prince, amongst other things, 'a fat Adonis of forty' – reflects the conventional liberal attitude of the time. His poetic observation of women, ranging from romantic idealization to cynical denigration ('Woman! When I behold thee flippant, vain'), and dwelling on physical externals in an old-fashioned way, can be comfortably perceived as adolescent. At this first stage his understanding and expression of the Romantic revolt against Neo-Classicism in thought, subject matter, language and poetic form seem to me conventional in their superficiality. Lastly, his aversion to Christianity, as first expressed in such a poem as 'Written in Disgust of Vulgar Superstition', a sonnet written in December 1816 while Sunday morning church bells were ringing, an aversion which was to stay with him until the end, also lacks the serious definition and consideration that one might expect from a qualified apothecary of twenty-one. Keats may have known the contents of the undergraduate Shelley's pamphlet, *The Necessity of Atheism* (1811), in which religious faith is dismissed as irrational, but the psychic energy he might have used on Christianity soon went into the excitement of composing poetic projections based on Greek mythology, and remained there.

Against these limitations should be set the points of Keats's growth. Chief of these is the sonnet which is generally regarded as Keats's first poem of consequence, 'On First Looking into Chapman's Homer' (October 1816). It records the aesthetic thrill that Keats, already an experienced lover of poetry – 'Much have I travelled in the realms of gold', as he states in the first line – felt on reading the Jacobean poet's translation of Homer's *Iliad* and *Odyssey*, having previously been familiar only with Pope's Neo-Classical version. Keats's powerfully graphic evocation of the first Europeans as they set eyes on the Pacific Ocean, to whom he compares himself as he first set eyes on Chapman's Homer, is trebly significant. It demonstrates his profound preference for Renaissance language and poetic thought over those of the eighteenth century. It demonstrates his initial mastery of the sonnet form, at a level far above that of the many occasional sonnets which, until April 1817, he was in the habit of dashing off. And lastly, it testifies to the growing absorption into his creative imagination of the world of Greek mythology.

Keats's early reading in such books as the *Classical Dictionary* of John Lemprière came suddenly to poetic fruition in the autumn of 1816, not only in the sonnet just mentioned, but also in the two long poems *Sleep and Poetry* and 'I stood tip-toe upon a little hill'. These are

17

That is typically ecstatic early Keats. The magical excitement of the images is there, though slightly vague, as the epithets 'wondrous' and 'dusky' may suggest, and it is as yet unenriched by the tragic misery of the human heart, which Keats valued as essential to a poet.

A critical catalogue of some contemporary poets is followed by such lofty but also rather vague idealization of poetry as

> . . . A drainless shower
> Of light is Poesy; 'tis the supreme of power;
> 'Tis might half slumbering on its own right arm.
> (235–7)

Keats asserts that poetry should be a friend 'To soothe the cares and lift the thoughts of man' (247). The poem ends with a description of the pictures on the walls, and with Keats waking to new resolve: *Sleep and Poetry* is the manifesto of an aspiring young poet.

'I stood tip-toe upon a little hill' is a lesser piece than *Sleep and Poetry*, just over half the length, and concerned with fewer matters; but despite its abrupt termination, it is perhaps better, because it celebrates one continuous process, while the several elements of the previous poem, richly developed though they may be, give a sense of recording unsorted fusions of experience. Like *Sleep and Poetry*, 'I stood tip-toe' takes its departure from Keats's experience of one day; it was in the summer of 1816, when he stood on Hampstead Heath, delighting in the natural scene. In the poetic enjoyment of nature, which occupies the first ninety lines, Keats shows the particularity of natural description which distinguishes his work from now on: consider his goldfinches:

> Sometimes goldfinches one by one will drop
> From low-hung branches; little space they stop –
> But sip, and twitter, and their feathers sleek,
> Then off at once, as in a wanton freak,
> Or perhaps, to show their black and golden wings,
> Pausing upon their yellow flutterings.
> (87–92)

Into this scene Keats fantasizes an erotic female presence with 'half-smiling lips, and downward look' – an image originating from his loving contemplation of his future sister-in-law Georgiana, which was to persist in his poetry – who gives way to the moon. The presence of Cynthia, who is not so named until later in the poem, evokes short impressions of four pairs of classical lovers, including Eros and Psyche, whose tale produces perhaps the most admired lines in the poem.

Psyche, in order to enjoy the god of love, had promised to receive him only in the dark, but her longing to see him triumphed, and a drop of oil from the lamp she was holding awoke him, and she lost him in the furious displeasure of Zeus:

> The silver lamp – the ravishment – the wonder –
> The darkness – loneliness – the fearful thunder;
>
> (147–8)

The poet's mind returns to the love between Cynthia and the mortal Endymion, which he sees as a conjunction which will inspire the healthy and the sick alike to become capable of poetry. Evidently, at this point in writing the poem, which he usually referred to as 'my Endymion poem', Keats decided that Endymion was to be the subject of a long poem of much greater scope, and so he brought this one to a quick halt:

> Cynthia! I cannot tell the greater blisses
> That followed thine and thy dear shepherd's kisses:
> Was there a poet born? – But now no more,
> My wandering spirit must no further soar.
>
> (239–42)

Psyche, in Greek the soul, which was often represented in art as a butterfly entering the created, or leaving the dying, body, came to be associated with love; and in that guise she remained in Keats's poetry, and was to be celebrated in the most sensuous of the Spring Odes of 1819. But Endymion was at once to become the hero of his longest poem.

Endymion

Having determined his destiny as a poet, and his desire to enter the Temple of Fame, Keats made up his mind to write a long poem. 'I must make 4000 lines of one bare circumstance and fill them with poetry . . . a long poem is a test of Invention which I take to be the Polar Star of Poetry, as Fancy is the Sails, and Imagination the Rudder' (*Letters*, 27). His 'one bare circumstance' was to be the legend which already lived in his imagination: the story of how Endymion achieved immortality through loving, and being loved by, the goddess of the moon. This poem was written against the clock in competition with Shelley, who that summer wrote the slightly longer poem, *Laon and Cythna* (later renamed *The Revolt of Islam*), and was the first to complete the assignment.

Shelley, whom Keats often saw at this time, influenced Keats's choice of the subject of Endymion in another way. His *Alastor* (1816) tells of an aspiring poet who feels himself to be an outcast; after wandering in search of an ideal love in the East, where he loves an Arab girl, he dies in despair. Alastor and Endymion are typical romantic heroes, questing in lonely suffering for the fulfilment of an ideal. But whereas Shelley's hero ends pessimistically, Keats makes his hero achieve perfect love, which optimistically symbolizes the poetic and personal destiny for which he hoped.

In this quest poem the search for love, the prime subject, becomes also the search for poetic power and achievement. The two continually reinforce each other, and in the end become one. Crucial in the whole process is the role of the goddess of the moon, who is not specified until line 592 of Book I. She seeks to fulfil her love for the mortal Endymion with a longing as passionate as that with which Endymion yearns for her. The unknown goddess of his dream in Book I, the beautiful girls with whom he engages in dreamed couplings throughout the poem, and finally the Indian girl of Book IV, with whom he instantly falls in love, only to be told that he must not 'impiously' take 'the earthly realm' that she represents, are all, in the concluding lines of the poem, revealed to have been Cynthia herself. Her black Indian hair turns to divine gold in a magical transformation, and she settles to enjoy her Endymion for ever. The erotic and the divine, with their complementary aesthetics, which have been interacting from the beginning, thus fuse to define and celebrate the Keatsian ideal which is inherent in the myth.

Edmund Blunden, in his edition of Keats's poems (1955, 108), quotes Robert Bridges's evocative description of the structure of the poem:

Keats was not making an allegory, but using a legend ... The four books correspond with the four elements – I. Earth; II. Fire [Bridges notes that though Fire has its 'proper home beneath the earth's crust', the underground action of Book II seems mostly to neglect the fact]; III. Under sea = Water; IV. Air; and these typify respectively – I. Natural beauty; II. The mysteries of earth; III. The secrets of death; IV. Spiritual freedom and satisfaction.

BOOK I

After the introduction, and its famous opening 'A thing of beauty is a joy for ever' – a thought Keats reinforced and developed in many poems, right up to *The Fall of Hyperion* – the poem moves straight to forested Mount Latmos, haunt of Endymion, where 'a venerable priest' (149) prepares to lead worship of the rural fertility god, Pan. The

Hymn to Pan (232–306) is the high point of the poem's opening, and is often considered to be a forerunner, in both structure and excellence, of the Spring Odes of 1819. In five roughly equal stanzas the worshippers call on the god in panegyric terms, and finally plead with him to be the means by which they may transcend mere earthly existence:

> . . . be still the leaven,
> That spreading in this dull and clodded earth
> Gives it a touch ethereal, a new birth;
>
> (296–8)

The worshippers dance and recall mythical events until, as Endymion sits trance-bound in yearning for his Cynthia, his sister Peona (an invention of Keats) appears to comfort him, and takes him by boat to her favourite island. There he confesses the cause of his misery (578–671): his dream of visiting heaven and kissing his moon goddess. Peona chides him for being concerned with dreams instead of with heroic action, in reply to which Endymion outlines his ideals of 'fellowship with essence' (779). Keats amplified this in a letter to Taylor of January 1818: 'the gradations of Happiness even like a kind of Pleasure Thermometer' (*Letters*, 59–60). These 'gradations' (780–815) begin with aesthetic identification with nature, move on to the appreciation of various kinds of music, and lead 'to the chief intensity' which 'Is made of love and friendship', love, of course, crowning all because it nourishes 'life's self . . . by its proper pith'.

Further defending his choice of love as the star to follow, Endymion tells Peona of two other occasions when he had visions of the enigmatic goddess who haunted him: once when he saw her face in a well and once when, following the lance he had hurled into the brook where it landed, a mysterious voice accused him of impiety and seemed to prophesy of love. In telling Peona, he responds to the accusation by resolving not to prosecute his quest in continuing misery, but to occupy himself instead with 'demurest meditation' (975). They step into the boat and leave the island.

Each of Endymion's responses to the various encounters in the poem is, like this one, an element in the continuous testing of the hero; and with each correct response, he can proceed to the next testing encounter.

BOOK II

Keats opens his second book with a further defence of 'love and poesy' as proper subjects of concern, as against military conflicts, adventures and 'the death-day of empires' (34), and rejoins his wandering hero at the significant moment when 'a golden butterfly', perhaps a soul, comes to lead him to a fountain beside a cavern mouth, where it vanishes. A naiad appears, to pronounce that Endymion must undergo prolonged travel and suffering before he can be taken 'into the gentle bosom' (127) of his love. His yearning returns, and in his suffering he calls on the goddess to help him; a voice orders him to descend through the cavern:

> . . . He ne'er is crowned
> With immortality who fears to follow
> Where airy voices lead; so through the hollow,
> The silent mysteries of earth, descend!
>
> (211–14)

The new ordeal he has to face among underground mazes and caverns leads him again to plead with his goddess to release him from his dark loneliness into the upper air, where familiar aspects of nature prevail, but she is silent. So he continues on his way, resolute, and is accordingly favoured with a sight of Adonis, recumbent among his cupids, one of whom tells him briefly of the wooing by Venus of Adonis – the subject of Shakespeare's erotic poem. Venus herself appears, to confirm the story and to promise Endymion happiness if he continues to obey 'the guiding hand that fends' him 'through these wonders for sweet ends' (575). Soon after Venus has gone, Endymion sees Cybele, mother of the gods, pass by in a chariot pulled by sleepy lions. He prays for deliverance to Jove, whose eagle carries him to a scented bower, where, as he falls asleep, he finds himself in the arms of his goddess. Their love-making stops short of consummation because she fears scandal in heaven at the loss of her chastity, but before she leaves him sleeping, she promises

> Aye, by that kiss I vow an endless bliss,
> An immortality of passion's thine.
>
> (807–8)

Endymion reflects on all that has happened to him; a 'humming tone' signals the arrival of the nymph Arethusa in her best-known form, that of an underground stream, which in answer to his prayer propels him upwards out of the underground world until he 'saw the giant sea above his head' (1023).

Even such a compressed account as that of Book II may explain why F. T. Prince, in his introduction to the Arden edition of Shakespeare's *The Poems* (1960, xxvii), calls *Endymion* 'a work of confused intricacy'.

BOOK III

This opens with an obscurely expressed outburst against contemporary authoritarian regimes with their 'baaing vanities' and their trappings, and moves into a supplicatory address to Cynthia, who sends down

> A moonbeam to the deep, deep water-world,
> To find Endymion.
>
> (101–2)

The moonbeam revives him, and he travels, on a sea-floor littered with old weapons and precious objects from wrecked ships, together with skeletons of humans and monstrous sea-beasts, to his next fated appointment. It is with Glaucus, the sea god whose story Keats adapted from Books XIII and XIV of Ovid's *Metamorphoses*. In Ovid, Glaucus asks the lustful enchantress Circe to help him to win the love of the nymph Scylla; Circe offers herself instead, and when Glaucus refuses her, Circe metamorphoses Scylla into a loathsome monster, to ensure that Glaucus ceases his love-quest. In Keats, Glaucus falls for Circe's charms; for that, like others who did the same, he is metamorphosed, but not into a beast. He becomes a hideously aged man, and when he finds Scylla, she is dead. The arrival of Endymion fulfils a beneficent prophecy: Glaucus becomes again a beautiful young man, Scylla is resurrected, and together they restore to life

> . . . all lovers tempest-tossed,
> And in the savage overwhelming lost,
>
> (703–4)

The host of reunited lovers rejoice in Neptune's palace and, noting that his Cynthia is not among the celebrating deities, Endymion swoons. In his trance he receives her message that she will soon give him his 'endless heaven' of love, and he wakes to find himself back on land.

BOOK IV

After a modest invocation to past poets – an invocation at the beginning of a book or canto in a long poem being customary – Keats shows Endymion at the moment of finding the Indian maid, with her 'curls of glossy jet' (60). She is 'panting in the forest grass' (59) 'with all her limbs on tremble' (103). She sings a lengthy song of sorrow, which is what she found when she looked for pleasure; and she begs him to solace her. He agrees to be her lover. 'Foot-feathered Mercury', the Greek Hermes, reviews, nineteenth-century critics of distinction, such as Matthew Arnold and the later Poet Laureate, Robert Bridges, established a consensus of rejection. But with its overcrowding of brilliant events, descriptions, yearnings and love encounters, and above all with its consistent process, through suffering and glimpses of perfect joy, towards resolution, the poem resists such rejection. For me, the poem is all worth reading, and especially for such things as the hymn to Pan, the phantasmagorical power of the description of Endymion's underworld adventures in Book II, and the whole story of Glaucus in Book III. On the whole, the love scenes in which Endymion (surely a guise of Keats?) figures tend to fail, for several reasons. The young Keats's view of his love objects is that they are beautiful and passively yearning, yet grandiose in their physical passion; in short, they function as they might in an adolescent's dream of wish fulfilment. Then there is, as for all poets writing about love, the problem of how to present love-making aesthetically. This was especially acute for Keats, in view of the excessive prudery of the immediately pre-Victorian age. John Jones, in *John Keats's Dream of Truth* (1969), justly observes, of a skirmish Keats had with his publisher on the subject: 'the literary roasting he endures from Taylor is that of the pornographic writer who has one thing to say and has to go on saying it, but printably' (137). The guardedness of critical response to *Endymion* may owe something to a puritanical element in the exercise of academic taste, an element which is easily embarrassed by strongly sensuous writing, whether the subject is love or something else. Byron's view of Keats's early poetry seizes on what he regarded as the special nature of the poetic processes displayed. In letters written from Italy in the summer of 1820 to his publisher, John Murray, Byron accused Keats of 'the Onanism of Poetry' and declared 'such writing is a sort of mental masturbation – f-gg-g his *Imagination*. I don't mean he is indecent' (*Byron: Selected Letters and Journals*, 1972, 273).

It illuminates the poetry of Keats, and of other Romantic poets, to ponder the antipathy between him and Byron, in the light of this remark of Byron's, which was of course in a private letter and not intended for publication. Keats, comparing his poetic processes with those of Byron, wrote, 'He describes what he sees – I describe what I imagine – Mine is the hardest task' (*Letters*, 314). The role of the imagination was cardinal to Blake, Wordsworth, Coleridge, Shelley and Keats, who all, in their individual ways, regarded it as the key to poetic truth. But Byron, despite his Romantic persona and occasional Romantic treatment of his poetic heroes, was rootedly Neo-Classical in his poetic taste. The contemporary poets he invokes in his dedication to

Don Juan, who he believes 'feel the inherent glow', are Scott, Rogers, Campbell, Moore and Crabbe (vii). He thought Wordsworth unintelligible (I, xc) and included this in his 'poetical commandments':

> Thou shalt believe in Milton, Dryden, Pope;
> Thou shalt not set up Wordsworth, Coleridge, Southey.
>
> (I, ccv)

It has been left to two twentieth-century critics, Christopher Ricks (*Keats and Embarrassment*, 1974, which is probably the best single book on the poetry of Keats) and John Bayley ('Keats and Reality', *The Chatterton Lecture*, 1962), to perceive and analyse the forceful originality expressed in the early poems, to the disconcertment of some readers. Both made a now famous point in comparing the portrait of the grieving Niobe of *Endymion* with the widely admired description of the goddess of memory, Moneta, as she laments the fall of the Titans in *The Fall of Hyperion. A Dream*, Keats's last long poem. Here are the two passages:

> . . . Perhaps the trembling knee
> And frantic gape of lonely Niobe –
> Poor, lonely Niobe, when her lovely young
> Were dead and gone, and her caressing tongue
> Lay a lost thing upon her paly lip,
> And very, very deadliness did nip
> Her motherly cheeks.
>
> (*Endymion*, I, 337–43)

> . . . Then saw I a wan face,
> Not pined by human sorrows, but bright blanched
> By an immortal sickness which kills not.
> It works a constant change, which happy death
> Can put no end to; deathwards progressing
> To no death was that visage; it had passed
> The lily and the snow; and beyond these
> I must not think now, though I saw that face –
> But for her eyes I should have fled away.
> They held me back with a benignant light,
> Soft-mitigated by divinest lids . . .
>
> (*The Fall of Hyperion*, I, 256–66)

Bayley notes the realistic observation of the earlier description of the grieving woman, centring on the 'vulgar' word 'gape' and what he calls 'the terrible disregard for itself of this face in torment'. In a passage on the 'romantic *correctness*' of the Hyperion poems, while greatly admiring the picture of Moneta, he remarks, 'In its admirable movement there is something withheld which makes us wonder if Keats has in fact anything to withhold.'

The reality of observation, supported by the use of strong common words which Bayley and Ricks admired, shows often. Keats's friends pleaded with him unavailingly to jettison words thought to be lacking in poetic decorum. For example, Woodhouse suggested either 'raise' or 'push' for 'bob' in the line 'Of dolphins bob their noses through the brine' (I, 311). And Keats was on dangerous ground when he made whales 'snort their streams' (II, 885). But the poetic quality of sheer physicality is always popping up in Keats, and it is an education to go along with it: consider his cupids,

> Rubbing their sleepy eyes with lazy wrists,
> And doubling overhead their little fists
> In backward yawns . . .

(II, 508–10)

In maintaining his position, Keats was nevertheless aware not so much of external criticism but of his own reservations, which were more cruel. In his exaggeratedly defensive preface to *Endymion* when it was published in 1818, Keats notes that the reader 'must soon perceive great inexperience, immaturity, and every error denoting a feverish attempt, rather than a deed accomplished', and accuses himself of mawkishness. The poem may indeed be regarded as apprentice work, but when allowance is made for its prolixity and its occasional engendering of embarrassment in the reader, it stands as a promising and substantial achievement. It justifies its length by its thematic development and accompanying atmosphere. Its repeated use of dream as a condition of heightened perception and experience acts as rehearsal for the profounder revelations of poetic dream in his later poetry. Through them, Keats makes his great gift: the enlargement for the reader of imaginative consciousness in a manner distinct from that of all other poets.

2. 1818 and *Isabella*

Between completing *Endymion* at the end of November 1817 and starting work on *Hyperion* in October 1818, Keats wrote surprisingly few poems, and of those, only *Isabella; or, The Pot of Basil* is substantial in length and stature. There are, of course, the intriguing short lyric 'In drear-nighted December', eight sonnets and the verse letter 'To J. H. Reynolds, Esq.', which are interesting for their thought rather than their distinction as poetry, as well as the songs written in Devon, two of which, 'Where be ye going, you Devon maid' and 'Over the hill and over the dale', light-heartedly celebrate erotic goings-on. But these were all written by the spring of 1818, which was followed by Keats's walking tour of Scotland with Brown, from June to August. They passed through the Lake District, where Keats was enthralled by the power and beauty of the scenery, but was disappointed not to find Wordsworth at home there. In Scotland, despite his efforts to celebrate in poetry such matters as his admiration of Robert Burns, his ascent of Ben Nevis and his visit to Fingal's Cave, his output was disappointing. A bright exception is the galloping 'A Song about Myself', composed off the cuff in a letter to his sister Fanny, who was then fifteen. It is a gem of family experience, full of fun and good feeling, which would adorn any anthology of light verse.

1818 may thus be regarded almost as a year of pause, though not quite a fallow year. It constituted a whole twelvemonth out of the three and a half years during which Keats was writing poetry; it was a breathing space which can perhaps best be understood by considering the huge leap forward evinced by *Endymion* before it, and the astounding quantity and quality of the poetry he was to write immediately after it, in 1819.

Part of the explanation of the comparative poetic barrenness may also lie in what the year brought to Keats from the summer onwards. *Endymion*, which was published in April, received hostile reviews in the *Quarterly Review* (April), the *British Critic* (June) and *Blackwood's Magazine* (August); J. G. Lockhart's review in *Blackwood's* was severe to the point of being abusive. There were sad developments in the lives of his brothers, to both of whom Keats was devotedly close. Tom, the youngest of the three, with whom Keats had spent March and April in

Devon, spat 'a leetle blood this afternoon' (letter to Reynolds of 3 May, *Letters*, 96). George lost his job and, with his wife Georgiana, left for America to try his fortune; Keats saw them off at Liverpool on his way to Scotland. Then, suffering from repeated chills and a chronic sore throat, which may have had some premonitory connection with the tuberculosis which eventually killed him, he had to break off his tour at Inverness and return to London, where he looked after Tom until he died on 1 December. Keats was certainly experiencing the 'misery of the human heart', which he instinctively felt was essential to his development as a poet. Indeed, during the two months leading up to Tom's death, he was actually working well on the first poem of his to be widely acclaimed by his contemporaries, the tragic *Hyperion*.

Keats's awareness of the dark side of life which threatens happiness, and his resistance to it, are expressed to his friend Reynolds:

> Still do I that fierce destruction see:
> The shark at savage prey, the hawk at pounce,
> The gentle robin, like a pard or ounce
> Ravening a worm . . . Away, ye horrid moods,
> Moods of one's mind! . . .
>
> ('To J. H. Reynolds, Esq.', 102–6)

In contrast, when in a frame of mind more responsive to what he conceived as his poetic destiny, in his sonnet 'On Sitting Down to Read *King Lear* Once Again', he affirms the result of 'humbly' essaying such 'bitter-sweet' as Shakespeare offers:

> But, when I am consumèd in the fire,
> Give me new Phoenix wings to fly at my desire.

(Uncharacteristically the last line, perhaps by a careless oversight, has an extra foot.) That sonnet is inspired by Shakespeare, but the next, 'When I have fears that I may cease to be' (which, with hindsight, we are inclined to read as prophetic), actually echoes the form of such Shakespeare sonnets as numbers 12 and 64.

The spring of 1818 produced *Isabella*. Developing a hint from Hazlitt, who suggested in a lecture on Dryden and Pope in February that a poetic translation of a serious story by Boccaccio, such as that of Isabella, 'could not fail to succeed in the present day', Keats, at first in collaboration with Reynolds but very soon on his own, composed his poem of five hundred lines on the fifth story of the fourth day in *The Decameron*. On this day, tales were told of 'those whose love had an unhappy ending'; Boccaccio's summary runs: 'Isabetta's brothers murder her lover. He appears to her in a dream, and tells her where he is buried. She secretly digs up his head and puts it in a pot of basil. For a long time she weeps over it every day, her brothers take it away, and soon after she dies of grief' (trans. Richard Aldington, 1930, 228). Three of Boccaccio's ten gruesome tales describe parts of a murdered lover being served up to the grieving girl survivor. Dryden had picked 'Sigismonda and Guiscardo', in which a possessive father sends the murdered man's heart to the girl in a gold cup. She resolutely and realistically defends her passionate action in taking a lover and, to spite her father, commits suicide in the 'noble Roman fashion'. Keats chose *Isabella*, and from the beginning of the poem represents his heroine as a gentle innocent overwhelmed by a tender passion, although in the original she is eager to experience love in the usual matter-of-fact style of Boccaccio's women. In the poem, but not in the story, both Isabella and her Lorenzo suffer pathetically before achieving their short consummation, and the pathos of Isabella's grief, from the moment of the murder, mounts until she dies of sorrow. The contrast between Keats and Dryden, in their choice and treatment of subject, is instructive, especially of Keats, who made the greater change of mode.

Keats's response to his subject is to identify himself, in all the power of his youthful romantic sensibility, with the nature of love and its tragic outcome, and at the same time, in three sections spaced through the poem, to explore his own predicament as a poet treating such a subject. In this latter guise he invokes Boccaccio (145–60) and twice (433–5 and 481–8) calls on the triad of Melancholy, Music and Echo to breathe 'syllables of woe' appropriate to the muse of tragedy, Melpomene.

Keats avoids mundane details of intrigue and seduction, which Boccaccio usually specifies. The place where Isabella and Lorenzo consummate their love is delicately described as 'a bower of hyacinth and musk' (85), and they are not caught flagrantly in the act of love by the brothers, as in Boccaccio. Then, the necrophilic element of Boccaccio's plot, the fondling and kissing of the decomposing head, is transmuted (401–32) into a ceremony of tender solicitude. The ghastly tale is made beautiful partly by the judgement of the poet concerning such love: Keats observes that although 'Too many tears for lovers have been shed' (90), yet

> . . . for the general award of love,
> The little sweet doth kill much bitterness.
> (97–8)

31

The pace of the poem is generally slow when love is the subject, as Keats luxuriates in the atmosphere of passion and pathos, but quick and economical when the actions of the brothers are narrated.

The tale is adorned with factors of permanence and regeneration, which work throughout the poem against the facts of loss and putrefaction, and Isabella's love strengthens because of her suffering even before she learns of Lorenzo's death:

> . . . a richer zest
> Came tragic – passion not to be subdued,
> (246–7)

Lorenzo's love for Isabella increases when he is a ghost because he sees that she is pale and more beautiful in her grief; she revives in strength when she tends his severed head at home; and the head, with herbs washed into it by her tears, perfumes the basil and makes it grow. And it comforts her that she

> . . . in peace
> Hung over her sweet basil evermore,
> And moistened it with tears unto the core.
> (422–4)

The brothers, who in Boccaccio behave as standard Italian avengers of family dishonour and have no apprehensions about their action until they are found out, in Keats are first of all dehumanized as grasping capitalists (in a passage much favoured by modern left-wing critics, 105–36), then have guilty nightmares, and finally, after discovery, are summarily dispatched 'With blood upon their heads, to banishment' (480). The concluding concentration is upon Isabella's decline and death, 'Imploring for her basil to the last' (498), and upon the memory of her love and suffering, which remains in the Florentine community as a song based on her words. The poem is a vivid example of the frequent conjunction, in Keats's poetry, of ideas of love and death and immortality.

Keats's friends thought well of the poem; Charles Lamb praised it extravagantly. The poet himself, a year and a half later, when preparing it for publication in the 1820 volume, came to regard it as 'A weak-sided Poem' in which 'there is too much inexperience of life, and simplicity of knowledge' (letter to Woodhouse of 22 September 1819, Gittings, 298). It is not clear to me exactly what he meant by that; it seems that Keats was retrospectively embarrassed by what he perceived as a sentimentality which belonged to his earlier poetry. All the same, he remained true to the feeling of the poem. In a letter to Fanny Brawne, probably written soon after the lung haemorrhage in February 1820 which he rightly took as his death warrant (*Letters*, 356), he identified with the ghost of Lorenzo in his predicament:

In my present state of Health I feel too much separated from you and could almost speak to you in the words of Lorenzo's Ghost to Isabella

> Your Beauty grows upon me and I feel
> A greater love through all my essence steal.

3. *Hyperion*

In classical mythology Hyperion was a Titan, one of the earlier gods who under Saturn ruled the universe before being overthrown by the three sons of Saturn: Jupiter, Neptune and Pluto. He was a sun god, but unlike Apollo, who succeeded him, he had no special association with poetry and music. The fall of Hyperion, and its figurative significance in the scheme of things, began to fascinate Keats even before he had completed *Endymion*. The last words of his preface to the earlier poem state that he wished 'to try once more' to touch 'the beautiful mythology of Greece' before he bade it farewell; he had in mind the usurpation of the old gods by the brilliant young Olympians. It was to be a usurpation which would express his faith in the idea of progress and the inevitability of gradual betterment in human affairs. The old gods were magnificent and beautiful in their fall; yet, in being supplanted, they saw that their successors were more beautiful and were thus better fitted to rule. As one of them, Oceanus, puts it when recognizing the 'fresh perfection' of the younger gods,

> . . . For 'tis the eternal law
> That first in beauty should be first in might.
> (II, 228–9)

Keats began to write the poem soon after he returned from Scotland to nurse Tom, and had completed Book II by the time Tom died on 1 December. He abandoned it a few months and only 135 lines later, in April 1819, at the point at which Apollo, aware of the realms of suffering into which he has ventured, is declaring his own pre-eminence in an initiation ceremony with Mnemosyne, the goddess of memory and mother of the muses. The poem, which would presumably have gone on to represent Apollo's new order in some way, thus appears to be nearly complete, lacking only a rounding off; and yet, when published in 1820 it was entitled *Hyperion. A Fragment*. It was his first poem to be widely praised by his contemporaries: Byron and Shelley were most complimentary.

The reader who turns from *Endymion* and *Isabella* to *Hyperion* is at once aware of a huge difference of style. The movement of the verse is

34

weighty and graceful, the mode epic with an elegiac thrust appropriate to the subject, and the language lofty. In addition, the choice of blank verse as the metre freed him from the need to make any of the compromises of meaning which result from following a rhyme scheme. The entire poetic process is conducted with an elegant detachment new to Keats as, in the shadow of Milton and, to a lesser extent, of Dante, he aspires to, and largely achieves, the status of epic poet. He had been studying *Paradise Lost*, his copy of which, preserved at Keats House in Hampstead, he marked extensively; and his reading on his Scottish tour had been of Cary's blank verse translation of Dante's *Divine Comedy*.

The example of Milton was a cynosure for all the Romantics. Not only was he the greatest of English epic poets, but also the political and social views he advanced in poetry and prose were congenial to artists all over Europe who had lived through and after the French Revolution. Milton was a liberal and a republican who contended against religious bigotry at home and abroad; and after the Restoration, when the political system he had supported was largely destroyed and its surviving followers were persecuted, he heroically composed his masterpiece, though blind. Early in that masterpiece there figured a heroic rebel, Satan, whose response to being hurled out of heaven to everlasting torture was

> . . . What though the field be lost?
> All is not lost; the unconquerable Will,
> And study of revenge, immortal hate,
> And courage never to submit or yield:
> (*Paradise Lost*, I, 105–8)

Three elements often found in the Romantic sensibility were: philosophic opposition to tyranny of all kinds; idealistic figuring forth of political and moral systems superior to those of established current power; and acceptance of, even occasionally glorification in, the social and artistic isolation resulting from the stance poets and artists took. Romantic poets recognized them all in Milton, though in their epic creations they went against the true upshot of his two-pronged justification of the Christian establishment on earth, as celebrated in *Paradise Lost* and *Paradise Regained*. Shelley's *Prometheus Unbound*, which was subtitled 'A Lyrical Drama', though its scope and subject are epical, features a god who overthrew Jupiter in the interest of humanity, and offers a detailed vision of the enlightened dispensation which is to follow. With the overthrow of the tyrant god, Shelley sees man

> Equal, unclassed, tribeless, and nationless,
> Exempt from awe, worship, degree, the king
> Over himself; just, gentle, wise . . .
>
> (III, iii, 195–7)

In the superb lyrics in Act I, Shelley accords the arts as elevated a status in the new world as Keats does by raising Apollo to supremacy. But whereas Shelley offers a politically programmatic vision fuelled by a spirit of universal love, Keats adumbrates an artistic frame of mind which is creative on behalf of humanity because it is founded on wisdom and experience of suffering. This idea of suffering bringing wisdom and creativity develops continuously in Keats's work, and is as strong in the two Hyperion poems as it is anywhere. Perhaps the idealistic formulation would have been more explicit if he had completed the poem; but at least a concise explanation of why Apollo becomes a god with power is given shortly before the poem breaks off:

> Knowledge enormous makes a God of me.
> Names, deeds, grey legends, dire events, rebellions,
> Majesties, sovran voices, agonies,
> Creations and destroyings, all at once
> Pour into the wide hollows of my brain,
> And deify me, as if some blithe wine
> Or bright elixir peerless I had drunk,
> And so become immortal . . .
>
> (III, 113–20)

Keats's immediate debt to Milton, which is clear in the three-line list above, shows especially in the narrative structure of *Hyperion*. The subject of Book I is the benumbed suffering of Saturn and the other Titans (except Hyperion, who is yet to fall), and their partial recovery to action, just as Book I of *Paradise Lost* describes the agonies of Satan and the rebel angels in hell after they have been driven out of heaven. In Book II of *Hyperion* the Titans formally debate their predicament, as do the fallen angels in Book II of *Paradise Lost*; and each participant in debate, in both poems, is introduced with appropriate splendour.

The comparison should not be pressed too far. Structure is one thing, and subject another. The whole of Milton's poem deals with the fall and redemption of humankind as a triumph of God's purpose, whereas Keats's poem, in something like an allegory in which the gods represent human endeavours, narrates one stage in a cyclic process of improvement which is powered by intensity of aesthetic perception.

BOOK I

The poem opens with successive descriptions of two titanic deities, who in their mourning for lost empire are represented almost as colossal statues. If they move, it is a slow enormous gesture, almost beyond human body language. They are the fallen Saturn and his sorrowing wife Thea. First is Saturn, who by his despairing stillness clamps nature's vivid movements into hushed respect:

> A stream went voiceless by, still deadened more
> By reason of his fallen divinity
> Spreading a shade: the Naiad 'mid her reeds
> Pressed her cold finger closer to her lips.
>
> (I, 11–14)

To him comes his wife:

> Her face was large as that of Memphian sphinx,
> Pedestalled haply in a palace court,
> When sages looked to Egypt for their lore.
> But oh, how unlike marble was that face!
> How beautiful if sorrow had not made
> Sorrow more beautiful than beauty's self.
>
> (31–6)

Even time seems slowed down by the weight of their grief:

> One moon, with alteration slow, had shed
> Her silver seasons four upon the night,
> And still these two were postured motionless,
> Like natural sculpture in cathedral cavern;
> The frozen God still couchant on the earth,
> And the sad Goddess weeping at his feet.
>
> (83–8)

Saturn surmises that he has lost his identity 'Somewhere between the throne and where I sit' (115), which echoes the agonized predicament of the outcast monarch of *King Lear*, a play which Keats had reread while nursing Tom, and which remained for him a touchstone for the portrayal of suffering. Saturn's suggested remedy is like Lear's after his cursing of Goneril:

> . . . Thou shalt find
> That I'll resume the shape which thou dost think
> I have cast off for ever.
>
> (*King Lear*, I, iv, 305–7)

In accordance with Keats's poetic doctrine, the terms of Saturn's intention to restore his own power emphasize the aesthetic:

> . . . and there shall be
> Beautiful things made new, for the surprise
> Of the sky-children. I will give command:
> (I, 131–3)

Thea leads him towards where the massed fallen Titans have congregated, and attention switches to the as yet unfallen Hyperion, still riding heaven 'on his orbèd fire', the sun, but uneasy despite the incense rising from human worship at his altars. He shudders at the omens of his coming fall. Instead of blazing light, his palace glares 'a blood-red through all its thousand courts' (179), and the incense begins to 'Savour of poisonous brass and metal sick' (189), while his desperate 'wingèd minions', though hoping for deliverance, become at Fate's decree elements of the degenerative horror whom he sees as

> . . . spectres busy in a cold, cold gloom!
> O lank-eared phantoms of black-weeded pools!
> (229–30)

In his decline Hyperion breathes defiance:

> I will advance a terrible right arm
> Shall scare that infant thunderer, rebel Jove,
> And bid old Saturn take his throne again.
> (248–50)

His opposition takes the form of trying to use his sun-power to bring on premature dawn against the mists and clouds of the doom-portending night; and in a passage of considerable rhetorical splendour (251–304), the battle between his light and the conquering dark is waged, until at last he

> . . . by hard compulsion bent
> His spirit to the sorrow of the time;
> And all along a dismal rack of clouds,
> Upon the boundaries of day and night,
> He stretched himself in grief and radiance faint.
> (300–304)

Hyperion's father, Coelus, the Titan sky-god, comes to console him, and advises him to go down to earth to find Saturn. He leaves the sun in the care of his father, and 'in the van/Of circumstance' (i.e., the necessity of Fate) he accepts separation from the orb of his godhood's identity, 'And plunged all noiseless into the deep night' (357). So Book I ends with the two chief sons of Coelus, Saturn and Hyperion, the first long fallen and the second still struggling in his fall, launched on their separate ways to the place where the Titans have congregated.

BOOK II

In *Paradise Lost* Milton coins the word 'Pandemonium' for the name of 'the high Capital/Of Satan and his Peers' (I, 756–7). It means 'all the devils', and hence is a word we now use to describe any vast scene of disordered uproar. The student might well turn aside and look at Milton's colossal Chaos of liquid fire, volcanic violence and 'darkness visible', with its heaving turbulence of torment, in Book I to gain some idea of the scale of emulation that Keats required of himself. He wisely opted for a more austere 'sad place'; it was not to be an eternal base for evils assaults on the souls of earth's inhabitants, but a temporal collection point for defeated deities who, in their suffering, reflect ancient glamour rather than malevolence. The Titans, some of whom are listed in a Miltonic catalogue of strange names in lines 19–20, are described in various postures of torment in a dark landscape of crag and iron, where

> ... their own groans
> They felt, but heard not, for the solid roar
> Of thunderous waterfalls and torrents hoarse,
>
> (6–8)

It is an entirely barren place, with no blade of grass, or rooted growth, or soil to root in. There are impressive descriptions of individual Titans, such as

> ... Cottus; prone he lay, chin uppermost,
> As though in pain, for still upon the flint
> He ground severe his skull, with open mouth
> And eyes at horrid working ...
>
> (49–52)

This is very Miltonic in style, especially in the use and positioning of the adjective 'severe' as an adverb, and in the appearance of that favourite adjective of Milton, 'horrid', which is soon employed again.

The description of Saturn's arrival at the place, guided by Thea, evokes the size and mystery of the two Titans,

> ... who now had climbed
> With damp and slippery footing from a depth
> More horrid still. Above a sombre cliff
> Their heads appeared, and up their stature grew
> Till on the level height their steps found ease;
>
> (84–8)

Saturn opens the debate. He can see no reason for their plight, and asks Oceanus for help. Oceanus says that Saturn cannot perceive the truth, being 'King/And only blind from sheer supremacy' (185). The truth is that Saturn is 'not the beginning nor the end' (190), and that

> ... on our heels a fresh perfection treads,
> A power more strong in beauty, born of us
> And fated to excel us ...
>
> (212–14)

Oceanus ends his recommendation to Saturn to accept his deposition calmly by praising the beauty of his supplanter, the new god of the seas, Neptune:

> ... Have ye seen his face?
> Have ye beheld his chariot, foamed along
> By noble wingèd creatures he hath made?
> I saw him on the calmèd waters scud,
> With such a glow of beauty in his eyes,
> That it enforced me to bid sad farewell
> To all my empire ...
>
> (233–9)

Clymene, a sea-nymph, supports Oceanus. She tells how she was singing her grief into a sea-shell when, despite stopping up her 'frantic ears' against it, she was overwhelmed by a sweet voice heralding 'The morning-bright Apollo! Young Apollo!' But the note of realistic acceptance is challenged by 'the overwhelming voice/Of huge Enceladus' (303–4), the strongest giant among the Titans, who rouses them all to challenge the enemy

> And singe away the swollen clouds of Jove,
> Stifling that puny essence in its tent.
>
> (330–31)

Enceladus reminds them that

> ... Hyperion,
> Our brightest brother, still is undisgraced –
> Hyperion, lo! his radiance is here!
>
> (343–5)

But the fellow-god to whom they all turn in hope on his arrival, though still beautiful, is but 'a vast shade/In midst of his own brightness'- (372–3) and sighs, 'his hands contemplative ... pressed together' (377). He is defeated, and has accepted his defeat. Book II closes with the Titans in confusion, some dejected, some still furiously militant, with no way to express themselves but to shout defiantly, like mindlessly loyal armies of old, the name of their leader: 'Saturn!'

BOOK III

With Hyperion fallen, and the earlier battle between the Titans and Olympians not even figuring in the poem, the scope for further narrative development seems bound to involve only, or at the least, the triumph of Apollo. To return later to the account of the battle, as Milton did in Book VI of *Paradise Lost*, through the narration of Raphael to Adam and Eve, would not have been to Keats's purpose, seeing that the centre of his imaginative sympathy lies, for most of the poem, with the fallen Titans, and especially with Hyperion. Keats was faced with something like the same problem as Milton when, having accomplished two tremendous opening books about the suffering rebel Satan and his peers, the older poet for the first time is faced with the necessity of writing memorable poetry about God. Milton is commendably brief in presenting the unimpeachable authority and harmony of the Almighty:

> About him all the Sanctities of Heaven
> Stood thick as Starrs, and from his sight receiv'd
> Beatitude past utterance ...
>
> (III, 60–62)

Then God returns to the active debate – the justification of his action and the responsibility of the devils for their sin in rebelling.

For Keats, the triumph of Apollo is engineered by Fate, and his emergence into godhood is presided over by Mnemosyne. Though herself a Titan, her function as mother of the muses and goddess of memory allows Keats to give her a significant roving role. She witnesses the suffering of the Titans, then deserts them for Apollo; and, as the poem moves to the point at which it breaks off, she starts to prophesy the ascendancy of the new god, whose poetic function is emphasized by his possession of a lyre.

The 136 lines of Book III appear to have been composed laboriously, as if Keats lost impetus after his decision to move from portrayal of the old gods in their despairing mode, to justification of the new system. He expresses his wish to leave the Titans to their woes, and to invoke Apollonian instruments such as 'the Delphic harp' and 'the Dorian flute' on behalf of 'the father of all verse' (III, 1–13), that is, Apollo. In so doing he commits himself, perhaps without conscious decision, to abandoning the language which is right for Miltonic catastrophe, and to finding a language which is right for the exposition of the trinity of values represented by the take-over of Apollo: sorrow, wisdom, beauty, Whether or not that is true, the fact of the matter is that, with the exception of a few lines, most of the poetry in Book III is less magnificent, and less clear in meaning and purport, than the language of Books I and II.

The changed world of Apollo's ascendancy is evoked in lines of standard, if attractive, vague sensuousness:

> Flush everything that hath a vermeil hue,
> Let the rose glow intense and warm the air,
> And let the clouds of even and of morn
> Float in voluptuous fleeces o'er the hills;
>
> (14–17)

The luxurious vegetation surrounding Apollo fittingly contrasts with the utter barrenness of the suffering-place of the fallen Titans, but the luxuriance is that of some of the scenes in *Endymion*, and is described in similar language. The resemblance to the earlier poem is compounded when Mnemosyne appears, and Apollo asks her why he is so grief-stricken. The reader is inexorably reminded of the youthful suffering on quest of Endymion, for Apollo does not seem to be the kind of self-possessed master of Fate and beauty who declares a few lines later, 'Knowledge enormous makes a God of me' (113).

In the conclusion to the poem, written, according to Gittings (*LY*, 101), late in March 1819, the style returns to the imaginative grandeur of Books I and II. Significantly, Apollo's agony while experiencing the transition is expressed through a death simile, for Tom's recent death, and Keats's close involvement in all its circumstances, had left a permanent mark on his poetry: Apollo's 'wild commotions' were

> Most like the struggle at the gate of death;
> Or liker still to one who should take leave
> Of pale immortal death, and with a pang

> As hot as death's is chill, with fierce convulse
> Die into life . . .
>
> (126–30)
>
> During the pain Mnemosyne upheld
> Her arms as one who prophesied. At length
> Apollo shrieked – and lo! from all his limbs
> Celestial . . .
>
> (133–6)

At the point of this assumption of godhood, Keats's inspiration died. His original plan had been to proceed beyond the triumph of Apollo, by detailing the fall of each Titan, 'the main conflict between the new god, Apollo and Hyperion', and 'the second war of Giants against Gods' (Gittings, 484); but this could not be fulfilled in view of Keats's growing unease about what he regarded as a pseudo-Miltonic style.

In a last few words on *Hyperion*, it might be noted that in the role Keats prescribed for his Apollo, there are features and emphases which scarcely appear in the details of 'the beautiful mythology' on which he nominally based the work. That was bound to affect his confidence in the poem in process; one cannot use a myth as basis for a work and add, on any scale, meanings not inherent in the myth itself, unless at the outset one structures a thorough-going variation. The significant core of Keats's poem lies in the wisdom through suffering of Mnemosyne, who becomes the fructifying figure in his second attempt on his theme, *The Fall of Hyperion. A Dream*. There she takes her other name, Moneta, and, as a Keatsian composite of goddesses, who appears as a huge image soon after the poem begins, becomes a guide and interpreter to the poet in his dream quest (see Chapter 8).

4. Dreams through Stained Glass:
The Eve of St Agnes and *The Eve of St Mark*

The Eve of St Agnes

This narrative poem of forty-two Spenserian stanzas was written in one burst of a fortnight at the end of January 1819, when Keats was with Brown in Chichester and the nearby village of Bedhampton, ostensibly on holiday. The formal event of the poem is the carrying off of Madeline, a girl spellbound by the St Agnes' Eve legend, by her suitor, Porphyro, who penetrates the castle of her hostile family, and is helped by Madeline's old nurse. It is a much richer and more complex poem than Keats's previous verse tale of love, *Isabella*. Whereas the latter poem is restricted – successfully, in my view – to the expression of love pathos in circumstances of tragic horror, *The Eve of St Agnes*, in 'its romantic celebration of erotic fantasy' (Allott, 451), draws strongly on a literary tradition of medieval chivalry, richly embroiders the sexual dynamics and moral ambiguities inherent in the process of elopement, and places the whole sensual adventure in the quintessentially Keatsian world, in which the flawed ideality of dream and the hard truth of waking reality interact.

The subject of the poem was suggested to Keats by Isabella Jones, with whom he had a covert understanding at the time, though whether, as Gittings (*LY*, Chapter 6) proposes, they were the lovers of the poem, 'Hush, hush! Tread softly! Hush, hush, my dear', which was written the day before Keats started on *The Eve of St Agnes*, is uncertain. The legend of St Agnes, the patron saint of young virgins, was that on her Eve, 20 January, 'If ceremonies due they did aright' (50), girls would dream of their future husbands. The same superstition applied to St Mark's Eve (24 April), when a virgin may 'find her husband in the dark' at midnight, though the main legend of St Mark mentioned in connection with Keats's poem, which was written immediately after *The Eve of St Agnes*, is that people who keep vigil in the church porch three St Mark's midnights running 'will see the ghosts of those who are to die that year pass into the church' (*Brewer's Dictionary of Phrase and Fable*, 1989, 706a). Keats used the betrothal motif concerning St Mark eleven months later, but in a facetious way, in stanza lvi of *The Cap and Bells*.

The narrative of *The Eve of St Agnes*, moving as it does by nine-line verse paragraphs, each of distinctive content and atmosphere (see p. 138), is beautifully sequential, each element preparing for, and supporting, the central subject, which is the self-willed enchantment of Madeline and its realistic consequence – her enraptured deflowering and elopement with her lover.

Considering its subject, the poem opens with bitter contraries. It is the depth of a winter in which all nature suffers from the intense cold, and in which the only human at first is the Beadsman, an old pensioner who is paid to pray for the souls of the dead. The fire which might have warmed him has deliberately been reduced to 'Rough ashes', among which he penitentially prays for the redemption of sin (i–iii). It is all contrary to the warmth and essential youth of the love which is to be enjoyed. By his firm placing of the abduction in a religious setting, which is maintained throughout the poem, Keats faces and expresses the complexity of his subject: chastity, which is enjoined by the Church, is cold, while fulfilled love is hot. The Beadsman has not long to live ('already had his deathbell rung'), and the chapel aisle along which he totters is lined with 'the sculptured dead'.

That desolation of age and winter is immediately overlaid by the warmth of youthfully vigorous revelry, as the 'thousand guests' of the castle assemble to the din of 'silver, snarling trumpets' (31), and here, in contrast to the images of death in the chapel, the religious sculpture is aesthetically joyous. 'The carvèd angels, ever eager-eyed' have their 'hair blown back, and wings put cross-wise on their breasts'. But the assembly, whose presence is indicated throughout the poem by near- or far-heard music, spells danger to the invading lover, for, as we learn later, it is composed of 'the whole blood-thirsty race' of Porphyro's enemies (99). Everything in the poem is a matter of life and death; and that is a traditional factor of Romance. It is not just the Romeo and Juliet aspect of the story, in which Porphyro, like Romeo, dares his feudal enemies in order to achieve his love; for the lovers of Romance, it is always, though sometimes only metaphorically, life to have each other, and death not to do so.

Into this highly charged setting, Madeline is introduced (42), brooding on love and on what 'old dames full many times' have told her about the significance of St Agnes' Eve. In view of Porphyro's covert activities in her bedroom a little later, the important element in the 'ceremonies due' which Madeline must perform if she is to have a vision of her future husband, is the strict injunction not to look 'behind' or 'sideways' while performing the ritual, but to require 'Of heaven with upward eyes for all' that she desires (54). Deeply enthralled, in fact 'Hoodwinked with fairy fancy' (70), she is oblivious of every 'tiptoe, amorous cavalier' and the seductive music (60), and waits for 'the hallowed hour' (66). There Keats leaves her because, before she can retire 'supperless to bed' and there lie straight (a condition of the ritual which Keats renders as 'supine') and pray to her saint, her bedroom must be prepared, so that the vision vouchsafed by St Agnes may be turned into reality by the 'stratagem' devised by Porphyro.

The ardent wooer arrives outside the castle, taking care to be 'buttressed from moonlight'; his heart is 'on fire/For Madeline' (75-6). He prays for only the briefest contact with her, 'That he might gaze and worship all unseen' (80); and for that, or perhaps a single kiss, he risks death at the hands of the 'barbarian hordes,/Hyena foemen, and hot-blooded lords' (85-6). He gains entrance, and chances on the one person in the castle, besides Madeline, who is not hostile to him. The 'old beldame' Angela, in her function of co-plotter with the invading lover, reminds one irresistibly of the Nurse in *Romeo and Juliet*. But of course Shakespeare's creation, raunchy, vigorous and cynical, is far removed from Keats's conventionally Gothic nurse, who is fearful, and full of rectitude in agreeing to co-operate with Porphyro in his stratagem only if he will promise to marry Madeline. Keats's 'agèd creature', with her shufflings, her moral compunction, and her laboured provision of food and lute for Porphyro's bedroom escapade, dominates this relatively tedious part of the poem (xi–xxi), at the end of which the man is installed in his hiding place in Madeline's bedroom. At the end of the poem Angela, like the Beadsman, is savagely killed off, and both would have died in worse authorial dudgeon if Keats had not softened his conclusion. The accepted ending is

> . . . Angela the old
> Died palsy-twitched, with meagre face deform;
> The Beadsman, after thousand aves told,
> For ay unsought for slept among his ashes cold.
>
> (375-8)

The stronger draft which Keats intended to be included in the 1820 edition of his poems reads

> . . . Angela went off
> Twitch'd with palsy; and with face deform
> The beadsman stiffen'd 'twixt a sigh and laugh
> Ta'en sudden from his beads by one weak little cough.
>
> (Allott, 479)

Like the Beadsman, Angela knows her 'passing-bell may ere the mid-night toll' (156), and since she is by her own admission 'A poor, weak, palsy-stricken, churchyard thing' (155), it can at least be understood why Keats, who wished in any case not to leave his readers in too rosy a glow of love accomplished, used harsh disposal of the old – and, designedly, the religious old, to right the focus.

Only at the halfway stage of the poem does Madeline leave the festivities 'like a missioned spirit, unaware' (93), for her bedroom (which is discussed on pp. 138–9), and her arrival there is signalled and enhanced by the most gorgeous descriptive passage in the whole poem. It contains one of the many religious images, all strongly atmospheric, which Keats adapted from the impression made on him by residence near Chichester Cathedral and the nearby chapel at Stansted (see *LY*, Chapters 7–9):

> A casement high and triple-arched there was,
> All garlanded with carven imageries
> Of fruits, and flowers, and bunches of knot-grass,
> And diamonded with panes of quaint device
> Innumerable of stains and splendid dyes,
> As are the tiger-moth's deep-damasked wings;
> And in the midst, 'mong thousand heraldries,
> And twilight saints, and dim emblazonings,
> A shielded scutcheon blushed with blood of queens and kings.
>
> (208–16)

In the religious light of this casement, pink and silver by grace of moonlight and stained glass, Madeline, seeming 'a splendid angel' and crowned with a saint-like halo, kneels to pray to St Agnes in full view of the unseen Porphyro (219) before rising, in a sort of entranced meditation, to undress. Jack Stillinger, in his essay 'The Hoodwinking of Madeline: Scepticism in *The Eve of St Agnes*' (Hill, 144–68), penetratingly addresses this moment in the poem, and with a knowing sensibility stresses that Porphyro gains Madeline's bed only by a 'stratagem' – a word used twice in the poem. Voyeuristically, with Porphyro, the reader savours her nakedness as

> . . . by degrees
> Her rich attire creeps rustling to her knees.
> (229–30)

A moment later the entranced young man gazes 'upon her empty dress' (245), as the girl slips into a differently entranced slumber without having looked around her. Spying on involuntarily exhibited nakedness, a misdemeanour acknowledged even in classical mythology, which has Actaeon torn to pieces by hounds for gazing on chaste Diana's nakedness, is here excused. Or should the word be 'justified' or even 'recommended'? The justification would be Porphyro's above-board intention to carry Madeline off and marry her, using the stratagem of fulfilling in actuality the superstition associated with St Agnes.

It is the ritual of that fulfilment to which the poem now passes. As soon as Madeline is soundly in her 'azure-lidded sleep' (262), Porphyro emerges from the closet and lays upon a table covered with 'A cloth of woven crimson, gold, and jet' a feastlet of mostly oriental sweets displayed

> On golden dishes and in baskets bright
> Of wreathèd silver . . .
>
> (272–3)

He whispers to her in the conventional love terms which are so often drawn from religion:

> Thou art my heaven, and I thine eremite.*
>
> (277)

Pulling aside the curtains of the four-poster bed, he sinks his arm into her pillow; and at this point it seems that she accepts his presence as an event in her St Agnes dream, and so remains wholly unconscious until he wakes her with his lute-song, 'La belle dame sans mercy' (292). Her return to wakeful reality – 'Her blue affrayèd eyes wide open shone' (296) – is as sudden as that of Lucrece in Shakespeare's poem, who wakes to find Tarquin's hand upon her breast:

> She much amaz'd, breaks ope her lock'd up eyes.
>
> (446)

The cruel awakening in shock of Madeline leads pell-mell to the crucial events of the poem: Porphyro's taking of Madeline, her lament that, having betrayed her innocence, he will leave her, his reassurance on that point, and their safe departure together. This sequence, and particularly the first part of it (xxxiv–xxxvii), carries the deepest meanings of the poem, and is one of the clearest expressions of Keats's continual exploration of the nature of dream and waking reality, and their interaction.

Although Madeline is 'wide awake' because Porphyro has plucked

* 'hermit'.

the lute 'close to her ear', 'she still beheld ... the vision of her sleep', and that vision appears to be so strong that it holds her still in a half-waking state of agitation. She moans forth 'witless words' and looks 'dreamingly'. She is aware of 'a painful change', which relates to the difference between the Porphyro of whom she has been dreaming, with his 'looks immortal' and 'complainings [i.e. wooing speeches] dear', and the Porphyro of reality who kneels before her, 'pallid, chill and drear'. So diminished seems he that she fears he will die. Dream is glamorously stage-lit by the imagination; the awoken eye sees plain reality, which must be grappled with in terms of actual life.

As Madeline is jarred into wakefulness by his lute music, Porphyro assumes the religiose and statuesque posture of Lancelot at the bed of Guinevere – kneeling silent in worship before performing the act of carnal love. The 'smooth-sculptured' man will come to life when her declaration of love, disguised in the courtly convention as an admission of utter dependence on him, is made:

> Oh, leave me not in this eternal woe,
>   For if thou diest, my love, I know not where to go.
>
> (314–15)

Her signal galvanizes Porphyro: he rises 'Ethereal, flushed, and like a throbbing star'. Earl Wasserman (Hill, 126) glosses Keats's use of the word 'ethereal' as meaning the 'transfiguration of real things into values by means of ardor', and that fits a line the prime meaning of which is that the hero is ecstatically keyed up for the act of love.

The degree of physical fusion – and 'fusion' is the meaning of the word 'solution' in the following lines – the couple engage in seems to me to be well enough indicated in Keats's formal response to the problem as he wrote the poem in early 1819:

> Into her dream he melted, as the rose
> Blendeth its odour with the violet,
> Solution sweet ...
>
> (320–22)

But when, in 1820, Keats was preparing the poem for the press, he wished to sharpen the sense, just as he wished to dispose of the old more harshly (see p. 47), making it perfectly clear that Porphyro and Madeline make love before escaping. He proposed:

> So while she speaks his arms encroaching slow
> Have zon'd her, heart to heart ...

> With her wild dream he mingled as a rose
> Marryeth its odour to a violet.
>
> (Allott, 474)

It is only a slightly more specific poetic circumlocution, but Woodhouse and his publishers, Taylor & Hessey, were at one in rejecting both this clarification and the satiric hostility at the expense of the Beadsman and the beldame. Whichever version one prefers, one learns something from the comparison about Keats's state of mind as he proceeded to his foreknown death: he had become equally defiant in his celebration of sexual love and his despising of the ignominy of palsied death.

The certainty that Madeline has been deflowered rests in her immediately subsequent accusation:

> Though thou forsakest a deceivèd thing –
> A dove forlorn and lost with sick unprunèd wing.
>
> (332–3)

The dove in dishevel is an apt and not unusual image of betrayed virginity.

The swift escape of the lovers reads as a glooming triumph, a decisive rush across the menacing scenery of hostile reality.

> . . . aye, ages long ago
> These lovers fled away into the storm.
>
> (370–71)

The ending of the poem almost disallows the conventional ending that the lovers live happily ever after. The moon of St Agnes sets when the lovers' consummation ends, and they go out into the storm:

> 'Tis dark; quick pattereth the flaw-blown sleet.
>
> (325)

Its din and darkness help them to escape, past the enemies drunk asleep, the wakeful bloodhound beside the sprawling Porter, the hostile Baron and 'all his warrior-guests . . . long be-nightmared', and of course the dead and dying old.

The success of the poem arises from its richly suggestive imagery, often arranged in contraries, like the atmospheric components: the realistic din and uproar of the feasting castle, the quietness and entrancement of Madeline's myth-bound room; the external danger enfolding the tender excitement of the lovers; the cold outside, with its spiritual admonishment of chastity, and the warmth inside, also spiritual but applicable to sensual triumph; and the almost omnipresent music, its different qualities distributed to achieve precise atmospheric effects. 'Silver, snarling trumpets' welcome the arrival of 'the whole blood-thirsty race'; concealed outside the castle on his arrival, Porphyro hears 'the sound of merriment and chorus bland' (95); and, while he is setting out his ritual feast,

> The boisterous, midnight, festive clarion,
> The kettle-drum and far-heard clarionet,
> Affray his ears, though but in dying tone;
> The hall door shuts again, and all the noise is gone.
>
> (258–61)

The music which accords with the lovers' spiritual ecstasy is different: Porphyro takes Madeline's 'hollow lute, / Tumultuous' and plays 'chords that tenderest be', and Madeline, early entranced by the thought of the magical experience she is about to have, does not attend to 'The music, yearning like a God in pain' (56). That line, which occurs in an almost throw-away position in the poem (because Madeline 'scarcely heard' it), with its 'yearning' and 'pain' associated with a god, expresses the particular intensity for which Keats strove in his poetry. The beauty of art, the necessity of suffering, and the notion of the kind of divinity which the poet, like his created lovers, should strive to emulate, are all there.

The Eve of St Mark

Composed in the five days, 13 to 17 February 1819, this is an unfinished poem in octosyllabic couplets of 137 lines. Sixteen lines (101–16), in pastiche Middle English on the superstition concerning St Mark's Eve, were originally separate from the poem, and have been included in most texts only since H. W. Garrod's 1939 edition of Keats's poems. Nine months after abandoning the poem, Keats wrote of the possibility of completing it. He had written it 'in the spirit of Town quietude', but its incompleteness remained, to bother critics with its uncertainties and their own speculations about its true subject and likely direction if it had been persevered with. There is no mention in the poem, besides the sixteen lines mentioned, of any concern with the superstition about the vigil in the church porch on St Mark's Eve. On the contrary, Bertha, the central figure, is imaginatively busy reading 'the legend page / Of holy Mark from youth to age' (91–2), and, as the poem breaks off,

> . . . her constant eye had come
> Upon the fervent martyrdom,

> Then lastly to his holy shrine,
> Exalt amid the tapers' shine
> At Venice . . .
>
> (133–7)

So I follow W. E. Houghton (Hill, 168–83) in questioning the place of the sixteen lines in the poem; and I doubt the value of any hypothesis concerning what Keats did not write.

What we have is a charming fragment of Romantic self-indulgence in medieval atmosphere in which, free of the narrative particularity enforced in *The Eve of St Agnes*, Keats could express his enthusiasm for medieval Chichester and its environs, and at the same time include, obliquely, a reference to his relationship with Isabella Jones. It is a poem of serene tranquillity. There is no suggestion of a plot beginning except that, possibly, Bertha, by reading the 'curious volume patched and torn' (25), may be starting, being 'lost in dizzy maze' (69), to fall under a spell, like Madeline. Keats appears to have responded to his admiration of Chatterton by taking the name 'Bertha' from one of Chatterton's heroines, by writing in a metre Chatterton used, by treating a medieval subject, and above all by including in the poem a passage in pastiche Middle English (117–32) which is additional to the sixteen lines already mentioned.

The poem as it stands is composed of two lovely contrasted atmospheres, unconnected and unresolved on account of the absence of narrative. One is of the cathedral and its close, placed in the city and environed by the surrounding countryside (1–22, 42–7, 57–66); the other is of Bertha's room, which gives on to the Minster Square, and consists of the heroine, her movements among her furniture and her response to her book. Gittings (*LY*, Chapter 9) has shown that the gallimaufry of religious paraphernalia which perplexes Bertha as she reads about it (30–38) includes a description of the east windows of Stansted Chapel. And I think he may be right to suggest that the interior of the room, with Bertha in it, contains a memory of Isabella trying to read at night: she

> . . . struck a lamp from the dismal coal,
> Leaned forward, with bright drooping hair,
> And slant book full against the glare.
> Her shadow, in uneasy guise,
> Hovered about, a giant's size
> On ceiling beam and old oak chair.
>
> (72–7)

The Eve of St Agnes *and* The Eve of St Mark

Especially interesting is Gittings's surmise that the 'angled winter screen', with its depiction of exotic creatures, which seems out of place in the milieu of the poem, must represent a direct memory of such a screen in Isabella's house. Keats had mentioned the parrot in a letter to his brother George.

> The parrot's cage and panel square,
> And the warm angled winter screen
> On which were many monsters seen
> Called doves of Siam, Lima* mice,
> And legless birds of Paradise,
> Macaw and tender Av'davat,
> And silken-furred Angora cat.
>
> (78–84)

The interrupted poem is a serene and very Keatsian curiosity which gives considerable pleasure, though I think it has been overpraised.

* For 'lemur' – Keats's misunderstanding.

5. Death, Love and Fame: Shorter Poems from December 1818 to April 1819

The period between November 1818, when Keats stopped composing *Hyperion*, with only sixty or seventy lines to go before he finally abandoned it five months later, and May 1819, when he wrote his series of marvellous odes, is of peculiar interest, because during it he wrote poetry of two rather contrasting kinds. There are the lighter poems, mostly about love and poetic fame, which are serene and often playful, and written in four-stressed lines or in metres appropriate to song; one or two sonnets, fairy songs, and even three humorous Spenserian stanzas in praise of Brown. And there are the darker poems, which offer powerful expressions of love and of love's connection with decay and death, and also question the search for fame. *The Eve of St Agnes* and *The Eve of St Mark*, the subjects of the previous chapter, were composed in the middle of this period, and in their difference from one another express something of the contrast indicated here.

Contrasts of mood are evident throughout Keats's poetry, though perhaps they are not as marked elsewhere as at this time, when Keats was going through gruelling experiences which fuelled the intensity manifested in all his serious poetry from now on. On 1 December Tom died of tuberculosis only a few days after his nineteenth birthday, having been nursed by Keats for three months; that was a bereavement which Keats later said he would never get over. At the same time, on account of his medical training, he may well have recognized his own chronic sore throat, husky voice and chest constriction as signs of his having been similarly infected. At once his close friends, led by Brown, tried to distract him with a round of pleasure, which certainly produced some of the light verse. In late January and February his relationship with Isabella Jones reached its highest point, whatever that was; and then he never mentioned her again, though she remained a friend of his publisher; later Brown, as Keats's executor, gave her one of his books. Almost immediately, Fanny Brawne, who came to live next door, became the focus of his love interest. 'The Melancholy Storm' (Ward) and 'Dissipation and Darkness' (Gittings) are two illuminating chapter headings given to this period by biographers.

The lighter poems to be considered here are, first of all, 'Fancy' and the ode 'Bards of passion and of mirth', which are often thought of together, because both are written in four-stressed and predominantly trochaic lines, and were included in Keats's journal letter to his brother and sister-in-law in America, dated 16 December to 4 January 1819. He describes them as 'specimens of a sort of rondeau' in which he could amplify a single idea 'with greater ease and more delight and freedom than in the sonnet'. Neither of them is in fact a rondeau, which is a poem of ten or thirteen lines with repeating lines and only two rhyme sounds; but both have two characteristics of the musical rondo. That is to say, they deal each with a single subject, and contain the kind of thematic repetition which in music may recur several times. Something of the musical joy arising from coasting about a tune and then returning to an emphatic repetition of it is also in both poems. It is most marked in 'Fancy', which is more than twice as long as the ode, and is altogether a more substantial achievement. Both poems appear in many anthologies.

The ode 'Bards of passion and of mirth' is about the 'double immortality' of poets. They live posthumously in an Elysian heaven, which is detailed in the first part of the poem, but they also continue to live on earth through their works, which are described at the beginning of the second part as 'the souls ye left behind you'. The rather trite conclusion, before the repetition of the opening, is

> Thus ye teach us, every day,
> Wisdom, though fled far away.
>
> (35–6)

More interesting, in view of the title of Keats's longest and perhaps most intensely felt ode, which was to be written five months later, is the domination of heaven by the nightingale, which sings

> Not a senseless, trancèd thing,
> But divine melodious truth,
> Philosophic numbers* smooth,
> Tales and golden histories
> Of heaven and its mysteries.
>
> (18–22)

Although Barnard (99) calls it 'insipid', 'Fancy' seems to me better than that, because, albeit in fairly simple terms, it treats a problem Keats grappled with all his life: the value of the imaginative impulses

* 'verses'.

55

necessary for the creation of poetry, and the 'truth' of the resulting work. The very title presents modern readers with a problem, and it may be useful briefly to discuss how the overlapping concepts of 'fancy' and 'imagination' might have been thought of by Keats. 'Imagination' is the concept-forming and, in the poetic context, the image-creating, force of the mind which represents, or transforms, the realities of life as the poet experiences them: people, events, things in nature, thoughts. Shelley claims, in one of the lovely lyrics in *Prometheus Unbound*, that the imagination can lead the poet to a higher reality than that of actual observable life:

> He will watch from dawn to gloom
> The lake-reflected sun illume
> The yellow bees in the ivy-bloom,
> Nor heed nor see, what things they be;
> But from these create he can
> Forms more real than living man,
> Nurslings of immortality.
>
> (I, 743–9)

'Fancy', which operates as part of the imagination, is more capricious. *The Oxford English Dictionary* defines it (meaning number 3) as 'delusive imagination', which suits this poem most of the time. But Keats also seems to take advantage of a Renaissance application of the word in a song in Shakespeare's *The Merchant of Venice*, where it clearly means just the spirit by the activation of which love, or more particularly infatuation, is felt:

> Tell me where is fancy bred,
> Or in the heart, or in the head?
>
> (III, ii, 63–4)

> It is engendered in the eyes,
> With gazing fed, and fancy dies
> In the cradle where it lies.
>
> (III, ii, 67–9)

The poet-philosopher of the age, Coleridge, claims the primary imagination 'to be the living Power and prime agent of all human Perception', and the secondary imagination, which is part of the primary, to be the power which 'dissolves, dissipates, in order to re-create' (*Biographia Literaria*, XIII) and both these, too, fit the use of 'fancy' in the poem. But here Keats lays more emphasis on fanciful invention than on recreation. In Chapter XIV Coleridge brings both sets of ideas together in a definition which is appropriate for the study of Keats: 'Finally, GOOD SENSE is the BODY of poetic genius, FANCY its DRAPERY, MOTION its LIFE, and IMAGINATION the SOUL that is everywhere, and in each; and forms all into one graceful and intelligent whole.'

The poem opens with the establishment of Fancy more as a reality-escaping, than a reality-fulfilling, power, because, since 'Pleasure never is at home', Fancy must be allowed to 'roam'. If she is freed, or 'let loose' (9 and 67) as one of the refrain lines has it, then the man who exercises her will be showered with a cascade of various 'Beauties that the earth hath lost' (30). These natural beauties are joyfully catalogued, with Keats's usual uncanny exactitude and vividness of expression, until line 66, after which Fancy is envisaged as bringing to the man who exercises it a fantastically perfect and co-operative mistress. She again is a typical Keats creation, who exists in the same world of the imagination as the desirable goddess images of *Endymion*, and as Madeline in *The Eve of St Agnes*. But she has her own characteristics: her introduction is by means of the cynical 'Every thing is spoilt by use' (68) and 'Where's the face/One would meet in every place?' (73–4) – which leads to the playful creation of 'a mistress to thy mind' (80) by the power of Fancy, who now, as the epithet 'winged' suggests, becomes a sort of female Eros. The dream mistress will be as beautiful as Proserpine, but without the experience of suffering:

> Dulcet-eyed as Ceres' daughter
> Ere the God of Torment* taught her
> How to frown and how to chide . . .
>
> (81–3)

She will also be as alluring as the goddess of youth, because she has

> . . . a side
> White as Hebe's, when her zone†
> Slipped its golden clasp, and down
> Fell her kirtle to her feet,
>
> (84–7)

(Hebe, cup-bearer to the gods, 'fell down in an indecent posture as she was pouring nectar to the gods at a grand festival' – Lemprière, 265b). The revealed nakedness allows the presumed follow-up of love-making

---

*'Pluto'.
†'girdle'.

to be figurative of the mental action of the poet in enjoying the fruits of letting the fancy roam, by forcing her belt undone:

> Quickly break her prison-string
> And such joys as these she'll bring.
> (91–2)

The erotic has what will continue to be its usual place in Keats's declaration of his poetic faith, which is, that the creations of Fancy are wonderful to experience as art, but may be in doubtful relation with reality: Keats is always honest enough to fear that the ecstasies of the imaginative life may be delusive.

The six serious poems of this period to be discussed now include one of Keats's best-known poems, 'La Belle Dame Sans Merci'. The other five are all sonnets, of which 'As Hermes once took to his feathers light' is the finest, though, curiously, it is comparatively neglected. The first of these is the darkly contemplative 'Why did I laugh tonight?', which Keats included in the journal letter of 14 February to 3 May 1819, and for the strangeness of which, in sending it to his brother and sister-in-law, he offered something of a reassuring apology: 'Sane I went to bed and sane I arose.' In it Keats asks why he is capable of laughter since his 'human heart' is so concerned with suffering, in which love and the pursuit of fame through poetry provide the intensity necessary for fullness of life:

> . . . Oh, mortal pain!
> Oh, darkness, darkness! . . .
> (6–7)

> Verse, fame, and beauty are intense indeed,
> (13)

Keats apparently needed to reassure his family of his sanity because in the poem he positively entertains the idea of death as the culminating intensity of life:

> Yet could I on this very midnight cease,
> And the world's gaudy ensigns see in shreds.
> (11–12)

The last line places death as superior to 'verse, fame, and beauty', but textual variants express that superiority in different ways.

> But Death's intenser – Death is Life's high meed.
> (Allott, 489)

makes death the reward of life by reason of its greater intensity. The original text, in the letter, reads

> But Death intenser – Deaths is Life's high mead.
> (Gittings, 435)

That, as paraphrased by Barnard (159), means 'Life's high meed is ultimately claimed by Death, which is thus more intense than Life.' The thought expressed in this original, that Death, as the culminating intensity of life, must of necessity be faced, thus appears to qualify the potentially suicidal impulse of the earlier lines.

Keats's preoccupation with death, which is intermittent but intense from this time onwards, should not be regarded merely as some kind of expression, and extension into adulthood, of a typically adolescent, and typically Romantic, suicidal impulse or death-wish. To begin with, contemplation of death is common in poetry about love and fame, and has its place there because of the way that minds, and especially the minds of people capable of intense thought and emotion, work. Contemplation of the happy intensities of fully lived life, such as those of gratified love and artistic creation, characteristically produces contemplation and fear of the opposite, which is death. That is a psychological commonplace for which strong evidence is provided in – to give an unimpeachable example – Shakespeare's sonnets. In Keats's case this aspect is pragmatically exaggerated by the poet's medical and family acquaintance with death, and with his growing suspicion, which slowly developed into certainty, that his own death would not be long delayed. As early as *Sleep and Poetry* (late 1816) he expresses the preoccupation:

> Oh, for ten years, that I may overwhelm
> Myself in poesy; so I may do the deed
> That my own soul has to itself decreed.
> (96–8)

Gittings (435–6) argues that writing 'Why did I laugh tonight?' released something in Keats, so that he was able to compose the last sixty lines of Book III of *Hyperion*. He cites the repetition of the idea of darkness as evidence: the words of Apollo to Mnemosyne as he begins to take on godhood are

> . . . For me, dark, dark,
> And painful, vile oblivion seals my eyes.
> (86–7)

59

The sonnet 'To Sleep', which appears to have been composed at about the same time as 'La Belle Dame Sans Merci', is cast in the form of a tranquil prayer to sleep, in which the muffling repose of the desired state is gently enforced in almost every one of its smooth lines. That smoothness is scarcely disturbed by the definition of the pain of guilt that goes into the prayer in the last four lines:

> Save me from curious conscience, that still hoards
> Its strength from darkness, burrowing like a mole;
> Turn the key deftly in the oilèd wards,
> And seal the hushèd casket of my soul.

Two sonnets on fame, both composed on 30 April, reveal Keats advising himself how he ought to conduct himself in the pursuit of fame. The first, 'Fame like a wayward girl will still be coy' offers, in its concluding recommendation, a humorously detached defiance of a kind often found in Cavalier love poetry:

> Make your best bow to her and bid adieu –
> Then, if she likes it, she will follow you.

The obverse of that sonnet is 'How fevered is the man who cannot look', which expresses the exasperation Keats felt when he could not detach himself from the pursuit, and sensed that his urge was destructive of his personality and his poetic creativity: 'It is as if the rose should pluck itself'. His concluding advice complements that of the lighter poem which preceded this one:

> Why then should man, teasing the world for grace,
> Spoil his salvation for a fierce miscreed?

The sonnet 'As Hermes once' is not always given, as it should be, the helpful title it had on its first appearance, in Leigh Hunt's *Indicator* of 28 June 1820: 'A dream, after reading Dante's Episode of Paolo and Francesca'. It locates the lovers of the sestet, whose kisses Keats shares in his dream. In simple terms, the poem begins by welcoming poetic composition ('a Delphic reed') as a refuge from 'The dragon-world with all its hundred eyes'; a passionate claim to the right to privacy of Keats's essential self. Then the poet considers two poetic worlds as places of refuge, the first of which is rejected in favour of the second. This first poetic world is the classical, as represented by the story of Jove's striving to make love to Io (who is not named in the poem) despite the jealous overseeing of his wife Juno and her agent, the hundred-eyed Argus. The second world is the medieval one of Dante, as represented by the story of the poet's meeting in hell with the guilty lovers, Paolo and Francesca. Keats's dream refuge is therefore one of love as well as of poetry. Hermes's lulling of Argus was successful, so that Jove was able to relieve Io and fulfil his lust with her; and that, despite its fascination and satisfactions, Keats rejected, just as, in his candid letters, he so often rejected, with a keen sense of self-disgrace, his own masculine 'goatish, winnyish, lustful love' – a phrase he wrote in the margin of a passage in Burton's *Anatomy of Melancholy* (1621) about love as desire.

Keats's imaginative preference went to the poetic rendering of the experience of Paolo and Francesca, heroes of the episode which is still the best-known in Dante's *Inferno. The Divine Comedy*, in the blank verse translation by Henry Cary, had been Keats's reading on his Scottish tour with Brown in 1818, and in 1816 Leigh Hunt had published his poetic version of the Paolo and Francesca romance, *The Story of Rimini*. Before his fatal illness Keats, inspired by Dante, was learning Italian, and the influence of the thirteenth-century poet shows in other poems besides 'As Hermes once'. The story embraced by him as he read Dante is replete with the sweetness of irresistible adulterous love, the social condemnation and bewildered suffering arising from yielding to it, and the overwhelming pity that the predicament of the lovers aroused in Dante.

The events on which the poetry is based began with the bestowal in marriage of Francesca upon the deformed Gianciotto, son of the Lord of Rimini. Not surprisingly, she fell in love with his handsome younger brother Paolo. In1285 Gianciotto found them together and killed them, whence their presence in hell in the circle of the lustful, where they are blown about for ever in a black wind. The lovers had fallen into adulterous love by reading together the story of perhaps the most famous adulterers of romance, Lancelot and Guinevere. They put aside the book, and made love.

The ecstasy of the forbidden passion of both sets of lovers is caught by Keats in a letter to his brother and sister-in-law. He wrote that it gave him a dream in which, floating about in 'the whirling atmosphere' of Dante's hell, he experienced a warm and long-lasting kiss 'with a beautiful figure'; and he ended the account of his dream with the fervent, 'O that I could dream it every night' (*Letters*, 239). There is a terrible strangeness in Keats's conviction that there is ideal beauty in the forbidden love, not just on account of its essence, but also for the two associated reasons that it is full of suffering, and remains the private possession of the lovers who, despite being in hell, 'need not tell/Their sorrows'. Neither in Dante nor in Keats do penitence and guilt figure in the lovers' attitude.

> As Hermes once took to his feathers light,
>   When lullèd Argus, baffled, swooned and slept,
> So on a Delphic reed, my idle sprite
>   So played, so charmed, so conquered, so bereft
> The dragon-world of all its hundred eyes;
>   And, seeing it asleep, so fled away –
> Not to pure Ida with its snow-cold skies,
>   Nor unto Tempe where Jove grieved that day;
> But to that second circle of sad hell,
>   Where in the gust, the whirlwind, and the flaw
> Of rain and hail-stones, lovers need not tell
>   Their sorrows. Pale were the sweet lips I saw,
> Pale were the lips I kissed, and fair the form
> I floated with, about that melancholy storm.

This wonderful brooding sonnet epitomizes Keats's accomplishment in several ways. It draws on classical myth and a particularly lofty instance from the European medieval heritage, both of which are transfused with new meaning by imaginative power, and become essential to a personal emotional statement: love, as Keats experienced it, expresses its impetus in the context of sorrow, social rejection and death, and its ecstasy is the more intense because it is menaced by moribund decay, as represented especially in the repeated 'pale' in the closing lines. Lastly, its creative vision originates in dream, that transitional state, fertile for artists, between the subconscious and the waking consciousness. Dream, actual or simulated, is the characteristic creative condition on which Keats constantly drew. He repeatedly acknowledged this, and confirmed it once and for all in the title and substance of his last great poem, *The Fall of Hyperion. A Dream*.

And so to 'La Belle Dame Sans Merci', the title of which Keats took from an early fifteenth-century French poem by Alain Chartier. The phrase belongs to the terminology of courtly love, and describes a beautiful lady without 'mercy', that is, the sort of gracious kindness which prompts a woman to accept a lover's pleas. With its haunting medieval resonances, the poem is the last of those for which Keats drew on the literature and folklore of the Middle Ages. Much may be said of the sources of its ideas and images, but it is difficult, and perhaps unwise to attempt, to be specific about its final meaning. In this respect it may be approached and experienced in much the same way as Blake's poem 'The Sick Rose', which also raises, by powerful images and in even much briefer compass, ideas of love, corruption and death.

The narrative thrust of the poem places it at once as an evocation of the medieval supernatural ballad, one characteristic of which is the seduction by one of the faery folk of a human being, who loses his or her freedom or life in consequence. Such are Clerk Colvill, Tam Lin and especially Thomas the Rhymer, the last of whom was an actual poet of Erceldoune in Scotland who lived in the thirteenth century. The versification (see pp. 139–40) and the process of narration by dialogue show Keats to be deeply imbued with the spirit and techniques of the medieval ballad. Keats's first poetic master, Spenser, also wrote about enchantresses from the medieval worlds of ballad and Arthurian literature, one of whom, Duessa, figures strongly in Book I of *The Faerie Queene*. She may be a foretype of Keats's 'belle dame', who takes the power out of men by luring them into making love.

The further medieval reference in the poem concerns the idea of a waste land which might be made productive again by the action of a virtuous knight, as in the Grail legends. At the start of the poem the questioner of the haggard and woebegone knight-at-arms speaks in a winter landscape, from which the birds have departed:

> The sedge has withered from the lake,
>   And no birds sing! . . .
>
> (3–4)

> The squirrel's granary is full,
>   And the harvest's done.
>
> (7–8)

But, as she seduces the knight, La Belle Dame feeds him with such choice natural products as 'honey wild, and manna dew' (26). That plenty is part of the enchantment which lures him to the act of love, and to the ensuing sleep in her arms in which, with the sudden chill of nightmare, he

> . . . saw pale kings, and princes too,
>   Pale warriors, death-pale were they all;
> They cried – 'La belle Dame sans merci
>   Hath thee in thrall!'
>
> (37–40)

The 'horrid warning' uttered by the 'starved lips' of the nightmare figures – and 'starved' here means, as in Shakespeare, 'starved to death'

– confirms that the lady is a murderous enchantress. As the knight is seen by the questioner in a state of decay, perhaps because he was active and willing in his own seduction, it is suggested that he is responsible for the corruption of his essence, perhaps to the point of bringing on his death:

> I see a lily on thy brow,
> > With anguish moist and fever-dew,
> And on thy cheek a fading rose
> > Fast withereth too.

> (9–12)

The five-fold repetiton of 'pale' links the poem firmly with 'As Hermes once' in considering the act of love in connection with death. It is as if the knight was taken beyond life, saw in the hereafter others who, like himself, had been seduced by the enchantress, and was returned to this world weakened and corrupted past cure by his experience.

It seems that, whether or not the poem is an expression of Keats's guilt about love, it does present a complex image of his state of mind. Robert Graves expresses one view: 'That the Belle Dame represented Love, Death by Consumption ... and Poetry all at once can be confirmed by a study of the romances from which Keats derived the poem' (*The White Goddess*, 1948, 378). This idea of the enchantress being a sort of 'demon muse' is supported by Katherine M. Wilson in *The Nightingale and the Hawk: A Psychological Study of Keats's Ode* (1964); and there is some evidence from Keats's letters and our knowledge of his life to support Graves's opinion. Twice in his last two years, when desperately in love with Fanny Brawne, he put himself at a distance from her in order to make sure that he could concentrate on composing poetry; and that indicates strife between his two major impulses, which were to fulfil both his destiny as a poet and his love for her. Then, the connection between love and thoughts about death, discussed briefly on p. 59, is a permanent feature of Keats's cast of mind, and of his poetry.

Some of the images in the poem, including those of the rose and the lily, come from the section on Love-Melancholy in Burton's *Anatomy of Melancholy*, Keats's copy of which is marked accordingly. But all these ideas should be held in solution. It is the wholeness of the poem, with its hypnotically enforced suggestion and concentrated associations, which impresses itself on the reading and rereading of 'La Belle Dame Sans Merci'. It permanently haunts the mind with the music of its particular tragic themes, which need not be referred outside the poem itself.

After writing the poems considered in this chapter, with their inherent turmoil variously regarded and expressed, Keats launched without a break into the rapid composition of the poems on which, above all, his fame rests: the Spring Odes of 1819, all of which were written, as far as we can discover, in a mere three weeks.

6. The Spring Odes of 1819

The five odes are considered here in the conventional order, which is different from that on which Keats decided for the three he selected for inclusion in the 1820 volume of his poems. There the order is 'Ode to a Nightingale', 'Ode on a Grecian Urn' and 'Ode to Psyche', which, remarks Barnard, 'suggests a movement from doubt to affirmation' (108). Although it is generally agreed that 'Ode to Psyche' was composed first, there is less certainty that the next three were written in the order which I follow. Some doubt exists about the date of composition of 'Ode on Indolence', which reads, according to some interpretations with which I agree, as a kind of anti-climactic reflection on other odes, especially, 'Ode on a Grecian Urn'. Yet the poem definitely draws on something Keats wrote in his journal letter to America on 19 March, before writing any of the odes. Since all five were written in a short period, I think it best not to worry about the order, but rather to engage with the results of Keats's bewildering capacity to express different moods, even contrary ones, virtually simultaneously. Of that capacity, the time when Keats began to compose the Spring Odes is perhaps the best example of many. 'La Belle Dame Sans Merci' appears to be dated 21 April; the same day he wrote 'Song of Four Fairies', a poem a hundred lines long; and by the end of the month he had completed the sonnet 'To Sleep' (see p. 60) and the two sonnets on fame (see p. 58), as well as 'Ode to Psyche'.

An ode is the most exalted of the lyric forms of poetry. Poets who claim the definition and title of 'ode' for a work have generally respected such a categorization as that which opens the entry given in the *Princeton Encyclopedia of Poetry and Poetics* (1975, 585): 'the name for the most formal, ceremonious and complexly organized form of lyric poetry, usually of considerable length'. The word itself derives from an ancient Greek word meaning 'to sing' or 'to chant', and such a meaning was always reflected by Keats in the composition of any poem he designated 'ode'. (That applies to any ode discussed by me as 'Anacreontic' as well.) 'Complexly organized' in the above definition refers not only to the content and length of an ode, but also to its form, in which connection readers are referred to pp. 141–3, where the development of Keats's ideas about the stanzaic form of the odes, arising from his dissatisfaction with the rigidity of the two main forms of the sonnet, is discussed in some detail.

Not surprisingly, Keats was sparing in the use of the rather grand word 'ode', though such devoted contemporaries of Keats as Woodhouse, as well as a few modern critics, have been less punctilious. Besides the five odes in the chapter heading, Keats entitled as 'odes' only 'Ode to Apollo' (February 1815), 'Ode to May' (spring 1818), a fragment which he abandoned after composing one superb stanza of considerable intricacy, 'Bards of passion and of mirth' (December 1818), which is perhaps his only failure in intensity in this genre, and 'Ode to Fanny' (February 1820). Ode-like in tone and to some extent in mode, though not so entitled by the poet, are four passages in *Endymion*: the choric hymns to Pan (I, 232–306), Neptune (III, 943–90) and Diana (IV, 563–611), and the song to Sorrow (IV, 146–290). There are also 'To Apollo' (spring 1817) and, above all, 'To Autumn', which, though most critics have called it an ode, probably on account of its excellence and tone, Keats evidently did not think of as an ode, perhaps because its inception in his mind arose from a straightforward lyrical impulse.

In composing odes, Keats was identifying with a comparatively recent development in English poetry, which had begun after Shakespeare, with Ben Jonson and Milton, and had provided in his youth such fine Romantic exemplars as Coleridge's 'Dejection: An Ode' (1802) and Wordsworth's incomparable 'Ode: Intimations of Immortality' (published 1815). The latter in particular, with its lofty theme treated with passion, and its beautifully diverse and rhythmic stanza forms, was always there, from the time of its appearance, as a kind of guiding light to English composers of odes.

So, whenever Keats included 'ode' in the title of a poem, he was sure to feel passionate reverence for his subject, to adopt a lofty and musical tone in treating it, and to develop a special stanzaic form for it. The three subjects which consistently stimulated Keats to strain after appropriate loftiness were Apollo, who must be regarded as his tutelary deity, being the god of poetry; poetry itself, together with the idea of poetic immortality; and lastly, the girl he loved and wished to marry, his 'brilliant Queen' with her 'million-pleasured breast', Fanny Brawne. The exception to the rule that exalted respect is the right tone for an ode is the last of the five Spring Odes, 'Ode on Indolence', in which, pursuing a mordant strain of self-examination which is increasingly evident in his last year of poetic activity, he almost humorously seeks relief from the exigencies of maintaining poetic intensity. More of that later.

Although each of the odes is an individual poem, they may be perceived as complementary to each other, all being concerned with poetry as an art: its material, its images, the moods of its creator and its claims to immortality. Thus 'Ode to Psyche' draws on Keats's imaginative engagement with 'the beautiful mythology of Greece', to fancy the elevation of the mortal lover of god Cupid to godhood herself. Her temple, in the mind of the poet, will be dressed 'With the wreathed trellis of a working brain', so that she will preside over, and participate in, his acts of creation and love. 'Ode to a Nightingale' presents that familiar poetic bird as a type of permanence in art, viewed in the perspective of the poet's own creative mood, the rise and decline of which constitute the frame and determine the rhythm of the poem: his ecstasy in the halfway state between awake and asleep; his recognition of, and poetic profit from, the close relation between pain and pleasure; and his understanding of the contrast between the imaginary world of poetic ecstasy and the real world of suffering and death. 'Ode on a Grecian Urn' pursues the idea of the perfection and permanence of a fine work of art more selectively: the idealized ancient Greek life portrayed on the urn is frozen in an immobile eternity, with its narrative suggestions suspended in the moments pictured, and so is an example of unchangeable beauty and truth, which stands as a cynosure to all. 'Ode on Melancholy', the shortest of the odes, presents the mood of the title in one aspect following Burton, not as a spiritual vice, but as a rich state of mind in which intense feelings such as joy and 'aching Pleasure' may be expressed the more powerfully because of 'the wakeful anguish of the soul' in its melancholic state. 'Ode on Indolence' deals again with the idea of figures on an urn. They are three linked figures which Keats treats as personifications of Love, Ambition and Poesy; they change as he moves round the urn, and seem to be 'Shadows', 'Ghosts' whom, in his mood of indolence, he wishes to banish, that is, to cease being inspired by them.

In this century we have become accustomed to the idea that some of the best poetry may have as its subject poetry itself; and that is hardly surprising, seeing that poets are likely to write best on what they most care about; besides which, our age is thought to be more introspective than previous ages. Of many examples which come to mind, W. B. Yeats's two poems 'Sailing to Byzantium' and 'Byzantium' are probably the best known, and the ones which may be compared in some ways to Keats's Spring Odes. Both poets write about the nature of poetic artifice and create precisely formulated metaphorical schemes to express their hopes, their sense of achievement, and their sense of themselves in relation to the world they live in. But 'The fury and the mire of human veins', in the throb of which Yeats operates, are very different from 'The weariness, the fever, and the fret' of Keats's world of youthful death.

'Ode to Psyche'

The first of the odes resumes Keats's interest in the myth of Psyche, which he had already treated in 'I stood tip-toe upon a little hill' (see pp. 19–20). The poem enlarges the scope of the myth and, by making it more specific, shows the special attraction it held for Keats deepening. In particular, the mythological event which concludes the story of Psyche and is briefly indicated in lines 149–50 of the earlier poem is treated differently. In the original story – or rather the one chosen by Keats, because there are different versions of it – Psyche was punished first by Venus and then by Jupiter for her conduct with Eros, but in the end was pardoned by Jupiter and, though not accorded the status of goddess, was allowed to share the immortality of Eros. In the poem before us Keats, by a process to be described, launches her into the kind of immortality appropriate to a goddess, builds her a temple, worships her as her priestly hierophant, and consecrates her essential action, which is that of loving, together with the achievements of her fulfilment and happiness. The emphasis on this idea of Psyche, as deriving from the brain of the poet, confirms the judgement of Robert Graves: 'Keats's chief interest was the poet's relations with poetry, and the imagery he chose was predominantly sexual' (quoted by Kenneth Allott in Fraser, 202). By this analysis the story of Psyche, who proceeds through fulfilled passion and profound suffering to joyful immortality, becomes an extended metaphor for the making, and the career, of a poet. Keats seems to elect Psyche as almost a tutelary deity, another Apollo, but an internal one and a female one at that.

The poem first appears in the journal letter of 14 February to 3 May 1819 to George and Georgiana, soon after Keats's attack on the way Christianity regards earthly existence as a 'vale of tears'. For this concept, Keats proposes to substitute 'the vale of Soul-making', in which 'pains and troubles' are required 'to school an Intelligence and make it a soul' (*Letters*, 249–50). The soul thus created has capitalized its inherent 'sparks of divinity' and so is able 'ever to possess a bliss peculiar to each one's individual existence'. Accordingly, the Psyche of the poem may be seen as Keats's soul, as he wished it to be; and contemplation of such essential selfhood, in the guise of the story of Psyche, produces a serene joy. It is the happiest of the Spring Odes.

The poem opens with a short invocation to Psyche, which is followed at once by a questioning indication about Keats's familiar creative mood, which is characteristically between asleep and awake:

> Surely I dreamt today, or did I see
> The wingèd Psyche with awakened eyes?
>
> (5–6)

His trance-like state takes him to a secret forest place 'beneath the whispering roof/Of leaves and trembled blossoms' where he sees 'two fair creatures' who lie 'calm-breathing on the bedded grass', their arms and wings wrapped round each other. They have been making love, they will make love again as they wake 'At tender eye-dawn of aurorean love'; and their posture of peaceful (an important word for Keats when defining his mood during this period) intimate contact is an assurance of the eternity of their love. Their bower of love, as described by Keats, irresistibly reminds the readers of the 'Bower/More sacred and seques-tred' where Milton's Adam and Eve first make love:

> . . . The roofe
> Of thickest covert was inwoven shade
> Laurel and Mirtle . . .
>
> (IV, 692–4)

> . . . each beauteous flour
> *Iris* all hues, Roses, and Gessamin
> Rear'd high thir flourisht heads between, and wrought
> Mosaic . . .
>
> (IV, 697–700)

Eros and Psyche are both winged when represented in classical statuary, a butterfly image which Keats insists on here, but he withholds the identity of the lovers, with climactic effect, until the end of the first long irregular stanza or strophe:

> The wingèd boy I knew;
> But who wast thou, O happy, happy dove?
> His Psyche true!
>
> (21–3)

The second stanza resumes the invocational tone of the beginning of the poem, and expresses reverence for Psyche. She is praised as being more beautiful than the moon – here given the name of 'Phoebe', which emphasizes her brightness – and lovelier even than Venus, in her

form of the evening star, 'Vesper, amorous glow-worm of the sky'. Yet
she has none of the attributes of worship accorded these two goddesses:

> . . . though temple thou hast none,
>   Nor altar heaped with flowers;
> Nor virgin-choir to make delicious moan
>   Upon the midnight hours –
> No voice, no lute, no pipe, no incense sweet
>   From chain-swung censer teeming;
> No shrine, no grove, no oracle, no heat
>   Of pale-mouthed prophet dreaming.
>
> (28–35)

It is one of the most powerful of Keats's many evocations of ancient
Greek worship. Couched here in the negative, in the next stanza it
returns in the affirmative, with an effect like repetition in a sung prayer,
as a creation of the poet's adoring mind, which will rectify the negligence
of the ancients in failing to recognize her as a goddess:

> Yet even in these days so far retired
>   From happy pieties, thy lucent fans,
>   Fluttering among the faint Olympians,
> I see and sing, by my own eyes inspired.
> So let me be thy choir and make a moan
>   Upon the midnight hours –
> Thy voice, thy lute . . .
>
> (40–46)

The final stanza consolidates all the preceding affirmations with a
new and powerful fusion. The elements of natural beauty briefly mentioned in the first stanza and now immeasurably extended to include
'wild-ridgèd mountains', the floral tributes to Psyche's 'rosy sanctuary',
and the imagined ceremonies there, are bound together by the poet's
'branchèd thoughts', 'With all the gardener Fancy e'er could feign', to
make the perfect setting for Psyche to enjoy her divine immortality.
The crown of the poem is the return to the sexual image which, if
Graves's point be taken, expresses the ideal beauty and passion of
successful poetic creation:

> And there shall be for thee all soft delight
>   That shadowy thought can win,
> A bright torch, and a casement ope at night,
>   To let the warm Love in!
>
> (64–7)

The threatening mystery of the start of the old myth has been transcended: Psyche does not have to wait in darkness for the arrival of a lover she may not see, and whose beauty she may therefore doubt. Boldly, she holds a torch at the window she has opened, and can receive him in open warmth and certainty. That is the relationship Keats desired between his soul and his poetry; and it may be observed that, despite its specific ending, the poem's dominant mood is one of reverential awe at the prospect of immortal poetry, as evinced in the worship in Psyche's temple, rather than one of sexual excitement. Kenneth Allott (Fraser, 196) interestingly suggests that, for the poem, 'an architectural metaphor seems best, "Yes, I will be thy priest, and build a fane/In some untrodden region of my mind . . ." The poem itself is a Corinthian detail in the "fane" promised to the goddess.'

'Ode to Psyche' has been undeservedly neglected, compared with 'Ode to a Nightingale' and 'Ode on a Grecian Urn', but among its advocates have been two poets, Robert Bridges and T. S. Eliot. The former especially praised the final strophe, and the latter thought it the finest of all the odes.

'Ode to a Nightingale'

This is the longest and most personal of the odes. Indeed, leaving aside the ruefully light 'Ode on Indolence', it is the only one which is personal in an autobiographical sense. Whereas in the other odes, the images are created and examined as external factors with a life of their own, which are of high relevance to the poet's work, here the process of the poem, and its central subject, is the movement of the poet's mind, as sparked off by contemplation of what the nightingale means to him.

Since classical times the nightingale has been pre-eminently the bird of poetry and love, distinguished by its beautiful song by day and by night. In medieval bird allegory it stands for, and speaks for, passionate courtly love. In English Renaissance poetry the grisly classical myth of Philomela, who was turned into a nightingale after being raped and tortured, and achieving revenge for those horrors, serves increasingly to stress melancholy and suffering in connection with the love and beautiful song that the bird represents. The nightingale often figures in Shakespeare and Milton, and in Keats's own immediate forebears, Wordsworth and Coleridge. Keats probably knew Coleridge's two poems, 'To the Nightingale' (1796) and 'The Nightingale: 'A Conversation Poem' (1798); and only a few days before writing his own poem, on 11 April, he had walked on Hampstead Heath with the older poet, who had discoursed, more or less uninterruptedly, on many things, including 'Nightingales, Poetry – on Poetical Sensation' (*Letters*, 237).

Each of the poem's eight stanzas has a thematic core which, with the obvious exception of the first, is consequential on the preceding stanza, and then leads on to the next. An idea of the whole may be gained at once by placing the first and last lines of the poem together. It begins

> My heart aches, and a drowsy numbness pains

and ends

> Fled is that music . . . Do I wake or sleep?

Doubt, rather than certainty, about the trance-like state in which the poet feels and acknowledges his essential being, is conveyed by that flash of juxtaposition. It may be argued that doubt is more interesting than certainty; doubt requires continuing consideration, while certainty may inhibit further thought, and can only be celebrated.

The poem opens with the poet in a state of 'drowsy numbness', of the kind which might be induced by such a sedative as hemlock. It is the coming on of the creative mood, and it is not until line 7, when the 'light-wingèd Dryad of the trees', that is, the nightingale, is mentioned, that we know why the poet is completely entranced. It is 'not through envy' of the beautiful 'full-throated' song, 'But being too happy' in the happiness of the singing bird with which he identifies. There is a catch in the construction of the stanza, an anacoluthon of which the reader must beware: 'I' is the subject of the participle 'being', and the word, 'that', which begins line 7, means 'because':

> 'Tis not through envy of thy happy lot,
> > But being too happy in thine happiness –
> > > That thou, light-wingèd Dryad of the trees,
> > > > In some melodious plot
> > > Of beechen green, and shadows numberless,
> > > > Singest of summer in full-throated ease.
>
> (5–10)

The evocation, rather than the strict envisageable sense, of such phrases as 'melodious plot' and 'shadows numberless' creates in the mind the beauty of the song which, because of the clear musical meaning of 'full-throated ease', is readily accepted.

In the second stanza the dizzy bliss of the beautiful bird-song enjoyed in a state of drowsiness leads the poet to compare it with, and to yearn for, the compensations of intoxication. But it is about as far from befuddled drunkenness as can be imagined; it is a state of aesthetic exaltation consisting of the rich pleasures of an ideal Mediterranean life – a sensual Bacchic revelry governed by the word 'true', which establishes its validity: the carouse envisaged is one of the joys of reality:

> Tasting of Flora and the country green,
>> Dance, and Provençal song, and sunburnt mirth!
> Oh, for a beaker full of the warm South,
>> Full of the true, the blushful Hippocrene,
>>> With beaded bubbles winking at the brim,
>>>> And purple-stainèd mouth.
>
> (13–18)

The impressionistic style of creating atmosphere, noted in the first stanza, continues. Byron said he did not understand 'purple-stainèd mouth', and one can see why. Is it the drinker's or the beaker's mouth which is referred to? The same sort of question might be asked about 'sunburnt mirth'. Just as one might say of an Impressionist painting 'Let the (unrealistic) colours and shapes work on your mind', so one might advise the reader of such a Keats poem as this to 'Let the (elliptical) suggestion of juxtaposed word-ideas work on your mind'. It is the idea of a 'purple-stainèd mouth', and the conjunction of 'sunburnt' with 'mirth' that are important; the absence of literal sense reinforces the power of the image in each case. By these means the temptation for the poet to escape into a selected area of oblivion derived from reality is rendered powerful:

> That I might drink, and leave the world unseen,
>> And with thee fade away into the forest dim.
>
> (19–20)

(There is critical disagreement as to whether the hypermetrical alexandrine of the last line should stand. Allott, 526, notes that in subsequent transcripts and in the first published version of the poem the word 'away' was edited out, but the original draft includes it.)

The third stanza, in which Keats explores the happy consequences of being intoxicated, is in fact the low point of the poem. Intoxication will allow him to forget worldly wretchednesses which the nightingale has never known, such as

> The weariness, the fever, and the fret
>> Here, where men sit and hear each other groan;

> Where palsy shakes a few sad, last grey hairs,
> > Where youth grows pale, and spectre-thin, and dies;
> > > (23–6)

Above all, the world which can be banished by a wine-bibbing poet is one of horrible transience, where nothing lasts:

> > Where Beauty cannot keep her lustrous eyes,
> > > Or new Love pine at them beyond to-morrow.
> > > > (29–30)

The last line is especially significant: even suffering for the sake of Beauty and Love is curtailed by the abominations of time and decay.

That despairing prospect is at once rejected by the repeated 'Away!' at the beginning of the fourth stanza. The seduction of the nightingale's song must not lead to the concrete and sensuously inviting bubbles and beakers of Bacchus. The spiritual lethargy of that notion must be combated, and 'Though the dull brain perplexes and retards', the spirit of the poet must rise 'on the viewless [i.e., invisible] wings of Poesy'. The significant turn is to the mysterious beauties of nature at night, which are presided over by the 'Queen-Moon', whose light can hardly penetrate the thicket in which the nightingale sings. The sense of enchanted ecstasy deriving from the poet's determination is conveyed by one of Keats's most magical effects, the fanciful impossibility of

> > But here there is no light
> > Save what from heaven is with the breezes blown
> > Through verdurous glooms and winding mossy ways.
> > > (38–40)

Taking those 'verdurous glooms' as a departure point, the fifth stanza distils the perfection of nature on a dark night of May, as the poet contemplates his unseen surroundings to the accompaniment of the bird song. All around him fecund and beautiful flowers, grasses and trees are burgeoning and throwing out their colours and scents, as an evocation of the joy and mystery of the desired creative mood. I have always thought of this stanza as nature poetry not excelled elsewhere in Keats: no matter that, clearly in the mind that conceived it, lie the first few lines of Oberon's speech (*A Midsummer Night's Dream*, II, i, 248–67), in which he directs Puck to Titania's haunt, with its flower-list of violets, eglantine and musk-roses; and also the glimmering darkness of the balmy night in Coleridge's conversation poem. The senses of touch, smell, taste and hearing feed the imagination in the darkness, to induce

Critical Studies: The Poetry of Keats

a feeling of strong but tranquil exaltation. The trimeter of the eighth line signals the approaching conclusion of the stanza, which moves gently into the cadence of a new sound effect, undisturbed by the connective which in strict sense should introduce it:

> And mid-May's eldest child,
> The coming musk-rose, full of dewy wine,
> The murmurous haunt of flies on summer eves.
>
> (48–50)

The sixth stanza opens with the poet, as it were, standing back to contemplate the effect on himself of the lovely and serene stimuli of the previous stanza: 'Darkling, I listen'. His response to the perfection of this moment, which he believes will never be excelled, is to ponder death:

> Now more than ever seems it rich to die,
> To cease upon the midnight with no pain,
> While thou art pouring forth thy soul abroad
> In such an ecstasy.
>
> (55–8)

In psychology, it is known that a natural and quite common way for the human mind to work during utter living happiness is to think about the opposite, which is death. It is a response Shakespeare expressed in some of his sonnets, and perhaps his most moving exemplar of the phenomenon is his Othello, during the moment of his reunion with his bride, Desdemona, on the Cyprian quay-side:

> If it were now to die,
> 'Twere now to be most happy, for I fear
> My soul hath her content so absolute,
> That not another comfort like to this
> Succeeds in unknown fate.
>
> (II, i, 189–93)

Keats's cause is different but the thought is identical. All the same, as the sonnet 'Why did I laugh tonight?' (see p. 58) indicates, Keats often thought about death. It could hardly be otherwise in a young man, medically qualified, who had watched over the painful death of his mother and younger brother, the latter only five months before the writing of this poem.

But no more than Othello does Keats propose to follow out the

76

thought, and his voiced death-wish is dismissed as soon as uttered. It only *seems* 'rich to die', and the poet at once makes to himself the commonsense point that, if he dies, he will no longer be able to hear the nightingale's marvellous song, though it would continue, to begin with at least, as a requiem for his own death:

> Still wouldst thou sing, and I have ears in vain –
> To thy high requiem become a sod.
>
> (59–60)

That thought leads to the affirmation of Keats's constant wish: that art should be immortal. It is the nightingale's song that he is now considering in that light, but it probably in wish fulfilment foreshadows his own song, and in the seventh stanza, which is the last but one, he places the bird-song on successive stages of history, as immortal accompaniment to events of great importance or emotional significance. Since throughout the poem 'nightingale-song' is treated as a concept not inhering in a single short-lived bird, I think critical quibbles about the particular bird that Keats listened to should be ignored. 'Nightingale-song' was always there, and the implication of the historical review of its manifestations is that it always will be there:

> Thou wast not born for death, immortal bird!
> No hungry generations tread thee down;
> The voice I hear this passing night was heard
> In ancient days by emperor and clown:
> Perhaps the self-same song that found a path
> Through the sad heart of Ruth, when, sick for home,
> She stood in tears amid the alien corn;
> The same that oft-times hath
> Charmed magic casements, opening on the foam
> Of perilous seas in fairy lands forlorn.
>
> (61–70)

The progression is from serious and humorous social consequence, in the emperor and clown, to the human suffering of Ruth, from the well-known Bible account, and from that to a world which is clearly the province of a Romantic sensibility, that of Keats himself, as the adjectives 'magic', 'perilous', 'fairy', and 'forlorn' insist.

Arrival in this Keatsian world, after the prolonged exercise in poetic fancy which is the poem up to this point, is like the touch-down of an aerial machine on familiar ground: it does indicate the end of the poetic flight, the experience and consequence of which are the subject of the next, and last, stanza of the poem.

This eighth stanza is memorably connected with the magical world at the end of the seventh by the echoed word 'Forlorn', with its long vowel sound and almost spondaic effect, and the reverberation of its primary and secondary meanings. 'Forlorn', the surviving past participle of the now discarded verb 'forlose', means 'utterly lost' because of the intensive prefix 'for-'; the secondary meanings, which all flow from the primary one, describe the states consequent on being utterly lost variously, as 'desolate', 'hopeless', 'wretched' and 'forsaken':

> Forlorn! The very word is like a bell
> To toll me back from thee to my sole self!
> (71–2)

That is how Keats feels about the slow dying of the inspirational mood, a death which is signified by the increasing remoteness of the nightingale's song as the bird flies away. As he makes his adieux, he expresses his perennially nudging doubts about the validity of poetic experience as a component of real life:

> Adieu! The fancy cannot cheat so well
> As she is famed to do, deceiving elf.
> (73–4)

(The need to find a rhyme-word for 'self' has led Keats to the deplorable 'elf', which brings in a confusing irrelevance; it is rather worse than the weak rhyming of 'pains' and 'drains' in the opening lines of the poem.)

But the doubt, with the poetic infelicity included in expressing it, is only a grace-note to the final impact of the whole poem, which works as a celebration of the poetic mood and its productions. There is a kind of awed astonishment behind the accepting rhythm of the last lines, which return to the diminishing hauntedness of the nightingale's world of nature, now infused with the melancholy of the bird's 'plaintive anthem', before the grace-note of doubt is repeated.

> Adieu! adieu! Thy plaintive anthem fades
> Past the near meadows, over the still stream,
> Up the hill-side; and now 'tis buried deep
> In the next valley-glades:
> Was it a vision, or a waking dream?
> Fled is that music . . . Do I wake or sleep?
> (75–80)

That note of doubt constitutes an assurance that, wherever the poet's mind may soar, his feet will remain on the ground, where drugged oblivion must not be allowed to blur experience of human suffering and transience, and where the knowledge and acceptance of those gifts of fate and time are instrumental means by which the true poetic vision may be expressed and intensified.

'Ode on a Grecian Urn'

This poem and 'Ode to a Nightingale' are generally thought of together as Keats's best, some critics preferring one and some the other. Only the occasional critic prefers 'Ode to Psyche' or 'Ode on Melancholy', and I think all agree that the form in which Keats most distinguishes himself is the lyrical ode. Yet there appear to me to be four major differences between the two poems. 'Ode to a Nightingale' is a work of pervasive darkness (though we know from Brown that it was written in his garden one morning after breakfast) and mystery. There is no escaping the concatenation of 'fade', 'dim', 'here there is no light', 'glooms', 'I cannot see', 'embalmèd darkness', 'darkling', 'this passing night', 'death' and 'forlorn'. 'Ode on a Grecian Urn', in contrast, is continuously lit by the clarity with which a Grecian vase is illuminated in a museum for the benefit of the enthusiastic visitor who walks round it: each one of the scenes painted on the urn is picked out, as the brilliance of a poet's perception joins the brilliance of the implied clear line-drawing and Mediterranean sunlight – implied, perhaps, by the reader's knowledge of what a Grecian urn looks like.

The contrast between darkness and light is paralleled, in the conclusions of the two poems, by another and even starker contrast, despite the fact that the two poems are on cognate subjects. 'Ode to a Nightingale', for all its reverential commitment to its own poetic vision, ends in a heartfelt but circumspect recognition of doubt. 'Ode on a Grecian Urn', with all its dazzling visual detail intact, ends, at least superficially, in a strongly expressed certainty:

> 'Beauty is truth, truth beauty' – that is all
> Ye know on earth, and all ye need to know.
>
> (49–50)

The third contrast lies in the relation within the two poems of the poet to his work. 'Ode to a Nightingale' records a deeply personal experience, in which the use of the first-person singular forces the reader to share the suffering and aesthetic joy within the vision of Keats himself.

79

In 'Ode on a Grecian Urn' the poet has seemingly created an image of profound meaning which stands outside himself; he is not a character within the poem except insofar as its perceived creator may be seen to reveal his mind about his subject. There is no 'I' in the poem.

The fourth difference between the two poems lies in the treatment and function of time, which runs through both with differing though perhaps complementary significances. Though nightingale-song and the urn (a receptacle for the ashes of the dead) are both types of eternal beauty, standing for immortal poetry in some way, the former can be perceived only in the creative mood, which is fugitive and evanescent, while the urn, with its brilliantly pictured life, stands in eternal stasis to be contemplated at any time.

The four-line invocation to the urn is peculiarly dense in the best Keatsian style: a strong thrust dominates the metaphor which first defines the urn, combining ideas of active sex and virginity, and the definition, with its thought moulded by the intactness and survival through time of the artefact, is followed by the idea, modest for a poet, that narrative illustration such as that on the urn can tell a story better than a poem can:

> Thou still unravished bride of quietness,
>   Thou foster-child of silence and slow time,
> Sylvan historian, who canst thus express
>   A flowery tale more sweetly than our rhyme!
>
> (1–4)

The richness of suggestion is extraordinary. That 'still', besides its obvious meaning, can also mean 'stationary', like everything depicted on the surface of the urn; and why, since the word 'bride' has already taken the poem into personification, are 'silence and slow time' permitted to be only foster-parents and not real ones? Is it simply because they have fostered the urn through its centuries of preservation, or is Keats ensuring everywhere in the poem that intercourse does not take place, even in metaphor? The first of what appear to be three scenes depicted on the urn shows some kind of courtship dance going on, apparently with an orgy of love to follow:

> What leaf-fringed legend haunts about thy shape
>   Of deities or mortals, or of both,
>   In Tempe or the dales of Arcady?
>   What men or gods are these? What maidens loth?

What mad pursuit? What struggle to escape?
What pipes and timbrels? What wild ecstasy? *Dionysian*
(5–10)

The typically Grecian erotic ceremony is perfectly caught. There is no suggestion of the violence of rape; courtship in art is traditionally portrayed as convention in real life requires it to be: women begin by appearing 'loth' and struggling to escape, and then consentingly and happily join in the succeeding 'wild ecstasy'.

Possibly the subject of the second stanza, a youth singing to his girl to the accompaniment of pipe music, is picked out of the crowd in the first stanza; but more probably, it seems to me, the poet is looking at the next scene under the floral frieze that runs round the urn. It is a love-scene set to music, and is introduced by a conceit, to which imaginative people, including musicians and music-lovers, can well consent because it chimes with an aspect of common experience. It expresses the idea that one can imagine even lovelier music than any which one has actually heard:

Heard melodies are sweet, but those unheard
    Are sweeter; therefore, ye soft pipes, play on;
Not to the sensual ear, but, more endeared,
    Pipe to the spirit ditties of no tone.
(11–14)

Two favourite words of Keats's, 'sweet' and 'soft', establish the nature of the music: 'sweet' has been a word of blanket approval for any thing or person perceived as good or pleasant since Anglo-Saxon times, and it is the key-word for the first two stanzas, in which it occurs three times. 'Soft' usually carries an aesthetic as well as a sensuous meaning, and in *Lamia* as well as here is applied particularly to music.

The rest of the second stanza expresses for the first time the central truth about the urn, which was inherent in the very first line: the beauties and blisses depicted are frozen in immobility in poses of an anticipation which can never reach fulfilment. And the present picture of that is supplemented by another conceit, which complements the one with which the stanza opened. And again, the pondering mind can accept it, just as it can accept Robert Louis Stevenson's idea that it is better to travel hopefully than to arrive. The beauty of the song and the joyful anticipation of love, by being fixed in art, possess more purity and more power over the imagination than if they existed for only a stage in time, in process of fulfilment. The latter must involve change.

> Fair youth beneath the trees, thou canst not leave
> Thy song, nor ever can those trees be bare;
> Bold lover, never, never canst thou kiss,
> Though winning near the goal – yet do not grieve;
> She cannot fade, though thou hast not thy bliss,
> For ever wilt thou love, and she be fair!
>
> (15–20)

The third stanza, which remains with the picture of the second, further develops the thematic paradox which may be said to dominate the whole poem: perfect joy caught by art in a fixed moment gives a more ecstatic pleasure than the same joy experienced in real life as part of a process. Love and music happen through time, and so perfect joy will probably be left behind. The moment selected for this observation is that described feelingly in the previous stanza, with the emphasis this time on the girl, who is 'For ever panting and for ever young'. And a new key-word, 'happy', the repeated use of which has been thought weak by several critics, expresses and confirms the bliss six times:

> Ah, happy, happy boughs, that cannot shed
> Your leaves, nor ever bid the spring adieu;
> And, happy melodist, unwearièd,
> For ever piping songs for ever new!
> More happy love, more happy, happy love!
> For ever warm and still to be enjoyed,
> For ever panting, and for ever young –
>
> (21–7)

The rest of the stanza describes in explicit terms how sexual passion in real life is inferior to the depiction of it in art on the urn:

> All breathing human passion far above,
> That leaves a heart high-sorrowful and cloyed,
> A burning forehead, and a parching tongue.
>
> (28–30)

That invites acceptance, it seems to me, as the personal view of Keats, who nowhere in his poetry (except possibly in *Isabella*) celebrates the reality, as opposed to the dream, of a harmonious love relationship. It is as if conventional youthful frustration, three symptoms of which appear in the last two lines quoted, hinder him. At this point in the poem, it seems as if concentration on artistic beauty is a recourse of the poet with an element of relief in it. But the process of the poem is not yet complete.

The fourth stanza brings to the reader a new picture, the meaning of which is demanded, though with fewer posed questions than those excited by the agitated scene described at the beginning of the poem. It is of a sacrificial procession, with a priest at its head, leading the victim-beast to the altar:

> Who are these coming to the sacrifice?
>   To what green altar, O mysterious priest,
>   Leadst thou that heifer lowing at the skies,
>   And all her silken flanks with garlands dressed?
>   (31–4)

Keats has picked out of his memory a detail, probably from Claude's *Landscape with the Father of Psyche Sacrificing at the Temple of Apollo*, which he had mentioned in the verse letter written to Reynolds a year previously:

> The sacrifice goes on; the pontiff knife
> Gleams in the sun, the milk-white heifer lows,
> The pipes go shrilly, the libation flows.
>   (20–22)

In his renewed treatment of this extraordinarily rich scene – in which the epithet 'silken' indicates to me that he has actually stroked a heifer – the introduction of crowds embarking on a pagan rite contrasts strongly with the preceding scene of the two lovers. But Keats does not expatiate on, or rhapsodize about, the procession. Instead he takes us to a place not pictured on the urn, the 'little town' of uncertain location which has been 'emptied of this folk, this pious morn'. Its desolation, which must continue for ever, like everything else connected with the urn, is hauntingly celebrated:

> And, little town, thy streets for evermore
>   Will silent be; and not a soul to tell
>   Why thou art desolate can e'er return.
>   (38–40)

The absence of life in the town emphasizes the absence of real life in the urn itself. The town is doubly dead: it is not pictured on the urn, and its inhabitants have all left it. Allen Tate (Fraser, 159–60) thinks the poem should end here, since the paradoxes in the juxtapositions – life: art and love: death – are complete. If art, as represented by the urn and its pictures, is the ultimate consolation, it is also death, because it promises no movement.

But there is a fifth stanza, with a new movement of its own. The whole urn is reconsidered in a short summary, and challenged:

> Thou, silent form, dost tease us out of thought
> As doth eternity . . .
>
> (44–5)

But consideration of that idea leads to a chilling judgement: the urn is summed up in the next phrase as 'Cold pastoral!' It is the opposite of 'For ever warm and still to be enjoyed', which was Keats's fancy about the girl mentioned in the third stanza. Eternity, even in the form of a work of art, lacks the heat of direct life, though the soul may find it friendly in contrast to the woes of actual living:

> When old age shall this generation waste,
>   Thou shalt remain, in midst of other woe
> Than ours, a friend to man, to whom thou say'st,
>   'Beauty is truth, truth beauty' – that is all
>   Ye know on earth, and all ye need to know.

Fraser excerpts remarks by eight critics about the aphorism in the penultimate line. The debate centres on two concerns besides questions as to how the two lines should be punctuated: Does the urn speak all of them, or is Keats the maker of the final declaration? And: Does the assertion in the aphorism make complete sense, especially as a conclusion to this poem? I think the answer to the first question is that the urn both speaks the aphorism and recommends it by way of admonishment to everybody: 'ye' is of course plural. The second question is harder: I agree with William Empson (Fraser, 129), that the aphorism itself can be understood best if the reader is familiar with the way Keats writes about the relation between Truth and Beauty throughout the letters, and particularly with this: 'The excellence of every art is in its intensity, capable of making all disagreeables evaporate from their being in close relation to Beauty and Truth . . . What the imagination seizes as Beauty must be Truth' (*Letters*, 37).

'Truth' is one of those words which, although everyone knows its primary meaning, requires definition in context whenever it is used in philosophical or critical discussion; and that is often difficult. Empson, in *The Structure of Complex Words* (1951, 373–4), considers two what he calls 'forbidden ideas' which emerge from Keats's aphorism: 'that there are no ugly truths' and 'that all truths are pleasant'. He notes that Keats would certainly agree that 'we recognize truth through the sense of beauty or fitness', and consequently we may go even further towards such a formulation as 'receptivity to the outer life (truth) is what gives fullness to the inner life and control over it (beauty) – that is, the poet needs to experience his burning forehead and his parching tongue'. I am left with the idea that a state of truth exists when experience, whether in art or in reality, is recognized in its completeness for what it is. That meaning does not fully appear in the last two lines of the poem, but is implicit throughout: in the poet's aesthetic response to the beauty of the urn (which Empson, in his piercing and often playful style, calls a 'pot'); in his recognition that the eternal life of the 'cold pastoral' is static and therefore not only alive in art but dead in life; and in his realistic assessment of emotional life and its transience. The poet had an easier case to make in 'Ode to a Nightingale' than in 'Ode on a Grecian Urn', and it shows in the conclusion of the latter.

'Ode on Melancholy'

This poem is a concentrated expression of Keats's familiar belief about the necessary conjunction, for himself as poet, of pleasure and pain, of joy and sorrow, using analysis of the mood of melancholy as the means. Swinburne (Fraser, 48) considered 'Ode on Melancholy' 'the subtlest in sweetness of thought and feeling' of all the odes. Empson delivered a full and sympathetic criticism in treating the seventh of his ambiguities (*Seven Types of Ambiguity*, 1930, 214–17), of which it is an extended example because its 'perfection of form' and 'immediacy of statement . . . lie in the fact that these [the opposite notions combined in the poem, which Empson mentions earlier] are collected into the single antithesis which unites Melancholy to Joy'. Despite the high praise of these two critics, 'Ode on Melancholy' has generally been rated lower than 'Ode to a Nightingale' and 'Ode on a Grecian Urn', and this may be for three reasons: it lacks the steadily strengthening force which length gives to the other odes; the image in the second stanza which draws on Keats's immature attitude to love relationships is not as attractive as others; and the sheer neatness in conformity of the poem's antitheses, so valued by Empson, denies the possibility of the kind of fruitful ambiguity which so often makes a poem something mysteriously powerful to return to again and again. But its vividness and the evidence of the intellectual care that has gone into its clear thesis remain as sources of delight.

The poem opens with a warning against regarding melancholy as the mood of despair, defeatism and horror, as it has often been depicted in art (by Dürer, for example). A proposed first stanza, which Keats rejected before the poem was published, ran riot among Gothic terrors in Keats's imagination:

> Though you should build a bark of dead man's bones,
> And rear a phantom gibbet for a mast,
> Stitch creeds together for a sail, with groans
> To fill it out, blood-stained and aghast;
> Although your rudder be a dragon's tail
> Long severed, yet still hard with agony,
> Your cordage large uprootings from the skull
> Of bald Medusa, certes you would fail
> To find the Melancholy . . .
>
> (Allott, 538–9)

Happily he resisted that product and sensibly composed a more measured and insidiously personal stanza, placing the negative instruction in the first word:

> No, no, go not to Lethe, neither twist
>   Wolf's-bane, tight-rooted, for its poisonous wine;
> Nor suffer thy pale forehead to be kissed
>   By nightshade, ruby grape of Proserpine.
>
> (1–4)

> For shade to shade will come too drowsily,
>   And drown the wakeful anguish of the soul.
>
> (9–10)

The second stanza contains advice about what to do instead of yielding to black melancholy; 'the wakeful anguish of the soul' must be experienced:

> But when the melancholy fit shall fall
>   Sudden from heaven like a weeping cloud,
> That fosters the droop-headed flowers all,
>   And hides the green hill in an April shroud;
> Then glut thy sorrow on a morning rose,
>   Or on the rainbow of the salt sand-wave,
>   Or on the wealth of globèd peonies;
> Or if thy mistress some rich anger shows,
>   Imprison her soft hand, and let her rave,
>   And feed deep, deep upon her peerless eyes.
>
> (11–20)

The enriching power of true melancholy (I use 'true' as Keats would) shows at once in the way it is characterized as fertilizing rain, the floral and scenic consequences of which spread with a wealth of lovely images through seven lines. There follows the discordant love image which, however it is regarded, does conform to Keats's idea, expressed twice in his letters, that any manifestation of strong feeling or purpose, even if it is violent, has its own beauty. He says it of the passions aroused in a street brawl, but more sympathetically writes of 'a stoat or a fieldmouse peeping out of the withered grass – the creature hath a purpose and its eyes are bright with it' (*Letters*, 229).

In the third stanza feeling aroused by the images in the second stanza are analysed and approved. The 'She' of the opening line may at first be understood as the raving mistress but, although the apparent ambiguity is allowed to stand, 'She' is Melancholy itself, which Keats, following Milton (in 'Il Penseroso') among others, personifies as female.

> She dwells with Beauty – Beauty that must die;
>   And Joy, whose hand is ever at his lips
> Bidding adieu; and aching Pleasure nigh,
>   Turning to poison while the bee-mouth sips.
>
> (21–4)

The masculinity of Joy, followed by the 'aching Pleasure' which turns to poison, subtly introduces the rhythm of the sexual experience; ecstatic joy is succeeded by sadness. The image of love-making intensifies in the closing lines, and is rounded off with an assertion of the worthwhileness of such experiences of true melancholy, which can be had only by people of fine feeling:

> Aye, in the very temple of Delight
>   Veiled Melancholy has her sovran shrine,
>   Though seen of none save him whose strenuous tongue
>   Can burst Joy's grape against his palate fine;
>   His soul shall taste the sadness of her might,
>   And be among her cloudy trophies hung.
>
> (25–30)

'Cloudy trophies' is one of Keats's surprising and powerful conjunctions. In the classical world a trophy was a memorial celebrating victory in battle, consisting of garlands and such things as loot or captured equipment, and hung on a tree or pillar in homage to the presiding deity of the victors. But 'cloudy'? It seems to refer back to 'soul' as well as to other trophies won by Melancholy; and she, with the numinous power of 'her might', is implicitly recognized as the deity who presides over true feeling.

'Ode on Indolence'

The Anacreontic spirit of 'Ode on Indolence', though applied to subjects dear to Keats besides the usual Anacreontic ones of love and drinking, must be happily faced. The prevailing tone of self-contemplation is detached and slightly humorous, and reminds me of the mood of secure and rueful self-mocking of which John Donne and Ben Jonson had sometimes made diverting poetry two hundred years before. The idea of figures on a Grecian urn, which had been adumbrated in the early verse letter 'To J. H. Reynolds, Esq.' and had come to exalted fruition in the famous ode, returns. But the three Shadows, who are identified in the third stanza as Love, Ambition and Poesy, are only '*like* figures on a marble urn' and appear three times to fascinate the poet, fading after each appearance like ghosts. It is not clear from the opening statement whether the poet-dreamer thinks he is walking round the urn 'to see the other side', or whether the urn itself is revolving. The three named figures, who are posed 'With bowèd necks, and joinèd hands, side-faced', are familiar to us under slightly different names. They are Beauty, Fame and Verse from 'Why did I laugh tonight?' (see p. 58).

The three figures are 'strange' to the poet, who does not at first recognize them, but he at once chides them for so deceiving him:

> How came ye muffled in so hush a masque?
> Was it a silent deep-disguisèd plot
> > To steal away, and leave without a task
> My idle days? . . .

> > > > (12–15)

And this deception succeeded, despite the fact that the poet was inclined to the poetic mood: 'Ripe was the drowsy hour'. Here, as in 'Ode to a Nightingale', is Keats's specialized use of the word 'drowsy', to describe the creative mood between asleep and awake. But this time, because he is in a 'blissful cloud of summer indolence', the required ingredients of poetic inspiration are lacking: 'Pain had no sting, and pleasure's wreath no flower'. So why did the three return a second and a third time?

Not side-faced now, in the third stanza they face him directly and tempt him to abandon indolence – Love, the fair maid, 'Ambition pale of cheek' and Keats's 'demon Poesy'. But for him

> They faded, and, forsooth! I wanted wings,
>> Oh, folly! What is Love? And where is it?
> And, for that poor Ambition – it springs
>> From a man's little heart's short fever-fit.
> For Poesy! No, she has not a joy –
>> At least for me – so sweet as drowsy noons,
>>> And evenings steeped in honeyed indolence.
>>>> (31–7)

Indolence has even charmed the word 'drowsy' back to its conventional meaning, and the poet luxuriates in the wish to avoid inconvenient facts and hard thinking:

> Oh, for an age so sheltered from annoy
>> That I may never know how change the moons,
>>> Or hear the voice of busy common-sense!
>>>> (38–40)

In the fifth stanza, Keats admits that, despite his indolence, the many nature subjects of poetry remain in his dreams; but, because of Indolence, he is able to resist them:

> O Shadows, 'twas a time to bid farewell!
>> Upon your skirts had fallen no tears of mine.
>>> (49–50)

So Love, Ambition and Poesy are all female, yet in his present mood they are unable to raise him to poetic expression, and to put him in the posture of 'A pet-lamb in a sentimental farce', that is, a creature which expects to be pampered and praised. The three ghosts are advised to

> . . . be once more
> In masque-like figures on the dreamy urn.
>> (55–6)

The poem ends with a command of dismissal, which leaves Indolence firmly in the ascendant:

> Vanish, ye phantoms, from my idle sprite
> Into the clouds, and never more return!

The cheerful paradox of the poem is that Keats, though pretending to resist the stresses of pleasure and pain which go with the creative mood, makes a witty and penetrating poem out of what is ostensibly an uncreative mood. Not surprisingly, in a letter to Sarah Jeffrey, he wrote a little later, 'The thing I have most enjoyed this year has been writing an ode to Indolence.'

7. *Lamia*

This narrative poem of seven hundred lines, in two books (composed June to September 1819), represents a concentrated achievement of a new kind for Keats, who thought so highly of it that he placed it first in the volume of his poems published in 1820. In a letter to J. H. Reynolds of 11 July, when he had completed the four hundred lines of Book I, he claimed that in the composition of it, he had made use of his judgement more deliberately than he had done hitherto, and had great hopes that it would be popular. The changes of tone and poetic form discussed on pp. 144–6 aptly illustrate Keats's observation on his own temperament at about the time when he wrote 'To Autumn' two months later: 'Some think I have lost that poetic ardour and fire 'tis said I once had ... but instead of that I hope I shall substitute a more thoughtful and quiet power' (letter to the George Keatses, 17–27 September 1818, *Letters*, 322).

But however Keats's poetic discipline in the poem may be regarded, there is nothing unrestrained in the theme of the poem and its emotional treatment. *Lamia* is the third account of the kind of event which Keats placed centrally in his poetry: the sexual union of a mortal man with an immortal, or at least superhuman, woman, and it is the one with the most drastic upshot. Such a union seems to symbolize for Keats 'the human yearning to retain forever the apex of passionate intensity' (D. Perkins, 'Ambiguity of Theme and Symbol in "La Belle Dame Sans Merci" and *Lamia*', Hill, 189). In *Endymion* the outcome is bliss and eternity after suffering: not only does Endymion come into permanent happy possession of his Cynthia, but Glaucus is delivered by Endymion from his evil enchantment at the hands of Circe, and 'the Paphian army' of lovers resume their bliss. In 'La Belle Dame Sans Merci' the knight-at-arms is discharged back to the human world weakened, and although it seems clear that the Belle Dame is an enchantress, her beauty, and perhaps her love for the knight, appear as 'real' as the world of dream can permit. But Lamia is shown from the outset as a snake-transformed-to-lustful-woman, with attendant echoes of Milton's lost paradise and of folk superstition. Her love for Lycius, however intense it may be, is still mainly an escape from serpenthood. Her put-on human beauty is described as meretricious, her attitude to the matrimony that Lycius imposes upon her is one of frantic dismay, and her contamination of Lycius's moral essence is so complete that, at the withering glance of truth which darts from the eyes of the philosopher–teacher Apollonius, she is banished to her serpent identity and he succumbs to death. All the males involved in these affairs may be regarded as types of Keats himself, and at least the last of the females is connected in some way with Fanny Brawne. In a letter to her written in July, Keats confessed that he associated her with a kind of Lamia figure whom he had just read about in Henry Weber's *Tales of the East*. All the 'melancholy men' in one tale reach 'some gardens of Paradise where they meet with a most enchanting Lady; and just as they are going to embrace her, she bids them shut their eyes . . . and [they] find themselves descending to the earth in a magic basket'. The men are rendered 'melancholy ever after', and Keats commented: 'How I applied this to you, my dear; how I palpitated at it' (*Letters*, 269). The very word 'palpitating' is applied to the snake Lamia on the first mention of her. Fanny must have found it both strange and hard to bear the weight of such an association.

Keats took the main story of *Lamia* from Burton, whom he quoted in full on the subject in the 1820 volume of his poems. But the prelude to the poem, with the love episode of Hermes and the nymph leading to the transformation of the enchantress from a serpent to the beautiful young woman who will seduce Lycius, the Keats figure, derives from other mythological material. As rendered by Keats, this prelude complements the source tale, to give it a meaning beyond the conventional magic-with-implied-moral-warning recorded in Burton's account.

The message in Burton, 'Lamias exist, and you should not have sexual congress with one', is far too simple for Keats, who exercised his poetic imagination on the idea that sex would be extravagantly satisfying when aided by supernatural titillation, and was honest enough to assess such activity as likely to prove harmful. However that may be, the poem, the opening lines of which delicately place the events to be narrated far in the classical past, proceeds with lurid sexual suggestion. Hermes, the long-haired conductor of souls to the place of the dead ('psychopomp' is the technical term for the holder of this office) and famed amorist among the immortals, is hotly hunting a lovely nymph, 'to whom all hoofed satyrs knelt':

> . . . a celestial heat
> Burnt from his wingèd heels to either ear,
> That from a whiteness, as the lily clear

> Blushed into roses 'mid his golden hair,
> Fallen in jealous curls about his shoulders bare.
>
> (I, 22–6)

In his fruitless hunt, in which the word 'jealous' figures twice, he comes across 'a palpitating snake', which is described at first as something of a Miltonic personification of serpentine sin, and turns out to have 'a woman's mouth with all its pearls complete' (60). This creature, which some unexplained power holds in snake form against her will, has foreknowledge of Hermes's incontinent quest, and drives a bargain with him: if he will grant her 'whatever bliss' she can devise, she will tell him where the nymph is. Her bliss will be to

> . . . have once more
> A woman's shape, and charming as before.
> I love a youth of Corinth – Oh, the bliss!
> Give me my woman's form, and place me where he is.
>
> (I, 117–20)

He grants, and she at once opens his eyes to where the nymph is. Immediately this nymph, in words which exemplify the kind of periphrasis for the act of love which early nineteenth-century publishers and readers could accept,

> Bloomed, and gave up her honey to the lees.
>
> (I, 143)

Keats's significant comment, which follows pell-mell and is instructive of his whole cast of thought about love and loving, is:

> Into the green-recessèd woods they flew;
> Nor grew they pale, as mortal lovers do.
>
> (I, 144–5)

We have been here before: 'pale' is a key-word in 'La Belle Dame Sans Merci', and in 'As Hermes once' it represents or warns of death. Keats's choice of Hermes, a lascivious god with an important function in the death of mortals, as introductory to two poems, must be appreciated. Lemprière notes that Hermes was thought to be the father of Priapus, and was sometimes represented in statuary with an erect penis. Keats allows the bliss of Hermes to be without suffering or evil, because 'real are the dreams of Gods' (I, 127).

Hermes is now out of the poem for good. Lamia the serpent is left to undergo the process of change into a beautiful woman, which is full of suffering:

> She writhed about, convulsed with scarlet pain.
>
> (I, 154)

Her brilliant serpentine adornments of scale and colour fall off one after another, until

> Nothing but pain and ugliness were left.
>
> (I, 164)

The suffering, which in Keats's system is obligatory as a prelude to bliss, is transitional only, for at once Lamia becomes 'a lady bright'. Not only that, but despite being an operator in what we must call the world of black magic rather than white magic, she is

> A virgin purest lipped, yet in the lore
> Of love deep learnèd to the red heart's core;
> Not one hour old, yet of sciential brain
> To unperplex bliss from its neighbour pain.
>
> (I, 189–92)

Keats insists on her double nature. She is virginal, but also, as he indicates by his use of a common term in sexual slang, she is a 'graduate' in experience of love,

> As though in Cupid's college she had spent
> Sweet days a lovely graduate, still unshent,
>
> (I, 197–8)

It seems to me fair comment that in this kind of fantasizing, the youthful male in Keats wants to have it both ways.

Now that Lamia is freed from her 'serpent prison-house', she can waylay Lycius, and, as she pursues this purpose, her magical powers, which sustain her human, virginal appearance, are emphasized. Even in her snake form she had been able to send her spirit 'where she willed' in the thrilling sensuous worlds of gods and mortals. It had been in such a spirit-musing that she had first seen Lycius on the Corinth road, and fallen in love with him. Her new encounter with him is presented in part as the work of Jove in answer to Lycius's prayer at the sacrificial altar:

> Jove heard his vows, and bettered his desire.
>
> (I, 229)

Her beauty and musical salutation inflame Lycius to greet her as a goddess, and she uses his assumption to justify her minx-like refusal of his first proposition:

93

> Thou canst not ask me with thee here to roam
> Over these hills and vales, where no joy is –
> Empty of immortality and bliss!
>
> (I, 276–8)

Lycius swoons, 'pale with pain', and Lamia, using practised lures, revives him with a kiss. Then

> . . . she began to sing,
> Happy in beauty, life, and love, and everything,
> A song of love, too sweet for earthly lyres,
>
> (I, 297–9)

This was how La Belle Dame had lured the knight-at-arms, with 'a fairy's song'. Epithets of strongly erotic suggestion advance the process: the watching stars draw in 'their panting fires', and she whispers to him in a 'trembling tone' that she is not immortal but a human like himself. Keats approves the change of tactics in a comment which illuminates his views of both the constant imagined female immortal of his poetry, and the equally constant vision of a loving and essentially compliant girl in real life, as the word 'treat' in this passage implies:

> Let the mad poets say whate'er they please
> Of the sweets of Fairies, Peris, Goddesses,
> There is not such a treat among them all,
> Haunters of cavern, lake, and waterfall,
> As a real woman . . .
>
> (I, 328–32)

The plot develops with insistent magical suggestion; Lamia virtually spirits Lycius into the city of Corinth:

> They passed the city gates, he knew not how,
> So noiseless, and he never thought to know.
>
> (I, 348–9)

There follows the much admired short description of the opulent and lascivious city whose licentiousness Paul castigated in Chapters 5 and 7 of his First Epistle to the Corinthians. But commentators have been wrong to suggest that that reference was the one taken up by Keats, who firmly placed his tale in pre-Christian times and got his information about Corinth from entries in dictionaries of classical times. Before its total destruction by the Romans in 146 BC, Corinth was a powerful commercial port and a cult-centre of Venus, whose temples housed 'a vast number of courtezans'. Keats fills his Corinth with a mysterious sensuous latency:

> As men talk in a dream, so Corinth all,
> Throughout her palaces imperial
> And all her populous streets and temples lewd,
> Muttered, like tempest in the distance brewed,
> To the wide-spreading night above her towers.
> Men, women, rich and poor, in the cool hours
> Shuffled their sandals o'er the pavements white,
> Companioned or alone; while many a light
> Flared, here and there, from wealthy festivals,
> And threw their moving shadows on the walls,
> Or found them clustered in the corniced shade
> Of some arched temple or dusky colonnade.
>
> (I, 350–61)

With unerring dramatic instinct, Keats at once has the couple pass Lycius's 'trusty guide/And good instructor', Apollonius, in the street. Lycius tries to hide his face from the sage's 'quick eyes', and Lamia's hands sweat with apprehension. The conflict in Lycius is clear from his double reaction to the sight of Apollonius: though he calls him 'trusty' and 'good', he adds

> '. . . but to-night he seems
> The ghost of folly haunting my sweet dreams.'
>
> (I, 376–7)

That is to say, he fears the warning function of such a ghost, which reflects the truthful qualities of Apollonius, but, with his reservation of 'but', he tries to hold fast to the belief that his 'sweet dreams' are morally defensible, i.e., 'real'. Lycius, like his creator, thus doubts the reality, and hence the morality, of dream experience, and the upshot of the poem confirms it. The couple gain Lamia's magically created mansion without knowing whether Apollonius has recognized them, and the suspense of the encounter remains in the reader's mind until it is resolved in the last event in the poem.

Book I closes with Keats caustically tempting readers with the notion that, since nobody knows where the lovers are, their story might now be concluded happily, but affirming that in the interests of truth, it must continue:

> And but the flitter-wingèd verse must tell,
> For truth's sake, what woe afterwards befell,
> 'Twould humour many a heart to leave them thus,
> Shut from the busy world, of more incredulous.
>
> (I, 394–7)

Book II opens with related detachment, behind which lies a tortured ambiguity. To use a term connected with other kinds of enterprise, Keats seems to be thinking on his feet, as the move from materialistic cynicism, through appalled contemplation of luxurious bliss, to defiant doubt, indicates:

> Love in a hut, with water and a crust,
> Is – Love, forgive us! – cinders, ashes, dust;
> Love in a palace is perhaps at last
> More grievous torment than a hermit's fast.
> That is a doubtful tale from fairy land,
> Hard for the non-elect to understand.
>
> (II, 1–6)

The next development is startling. The god of love is presented as 'jealous grown of so complete a pair', looking on them 'nightly, with terrific glare', and the effect of the intense bliss that the lovers experience is that the man longs to relate his ecstasy to the real world outside his magical mansion, just as his creator longed to justify his poetical dreams in terms of reality. As he moves towards this concretization of experience, Lamia, enchantress of illusions as well as feeling herself to be his human lover, senses that he is going out of her control, and that he is deserting her. He presses his mastery without knowing that his impulse will prove to be suicidal: matrimony is what he proposes, and that is doubly disastrous to her. Firstly, a lamia cannot accept such a social bonding as marriage, since her essential activities and satisfactions derive in their nature from unheavenly sexual domination; and secondly, the public manifestations of matrimony expose and thus smash the secrecy and illusion upon which her magic subsists. She kneels before him, 'Beseeching him ... to change his purpose', but he glories perversely in his mastery and

> ... in self-despite,
> Against his better self, he took delight
> Luxurious in her sorrows, soft and new.
>
> (II, 72–4)

The cruelty with which Lycius enforces his aim is given Keats's approval in a letter to Taylor: 'Women love to be forced to do a thing, by a fine fellow – *such as this*.' No member of Keats's publishing group thought anything wrong or worth censoring in this part of the poem; which means that the poet is in harmony with the general ideas of the Romantic period. Passionate and tender women are to be 'subdued' in fulfilment of the 'Fierce and sanguineous' (II, 76) desires of the men who love them. So, in the poem, Lamia emotionally sloughs off her serpent nature and behaves like a submissive human woman of Keats's imagination:

> . . . She burnt, she loved the tyranny,
> And, all subdued, consented to the hour
> When to the bridal he should lead his paramour.
> (II, 81–3)

It is one of the moments in the poem when the reader, besides questioning the drift of Keats's motivation in matters of sexual relationship, sympathizes with a lamia who tries her hardest to escape from her infernal nature into passive human love.

As the pair discuss their wedding arrangements, Lamia has to explain, by a pathetic lie, why she has neither relatives nor friends to invite:

> My parents' bones are in their dusty urns
> Sepulchred where no kindled incense burns,
> Seeing all their luckless race are dead, save me,
> And I neglect the holy rite for thee.
> (II, 94–7)

She begs him not to include Apollonius on the guest list, and when he asks why not, she feigns sleep and enchants him into deep slumber. Further magic is required to compensate for her inability to follow custom and to be brought

> . . . from home at blushing shut of day,
> Veiled, in a chariot, heralded along
> By strewn flowers, torches, and a marriage song.
> (II, 107–9)

She sets herself 'how to dress / The misery in fit magnificence' and conjures up supernatural servitors who, to the sound of 'haunting music', lay out a luxurious banquet under the 'fairy-roof'. The description should be compared and contrasted with that of Porphyro laying out his meal before the dreaming Madeline in *The Eve of St Agnes*: compared because of its equally rich sensuousness, contrasted because Keats infuses this description with a curious double sense of doom and false sanctity. The wine has come from 'the gloomy tun', and the conclusion is:

> Thus loaded with a feast the tables stood,
> Each shrining in the midst the image of a God.
>
> (II, 189–90)

To this scene of high luxury, with its promise of utmost feasting delight, the white-robed guests enter wonderingly. Among them is the uninvited Apollonius, who meets Lycius in the vestibule, where he justifies his gate-crashing on the grounds of inner compulsion, and requires Lycius to forgive him:

> '. . . yet must I do this wrong,
> And you forgive me.' . . .
>
> (II, 168–9)

Lycius responds

> With reconciling words and courteous mien
> Turning into sweet milk the sophist's spleen.
>
> (II, 171–2)

The coming catastrophe has its setting.

The curious tension in the poem between sensuous abandon and satiric detachment, which has been intermittently observable from the very beginning, continues. In a draft apparently jettisoned only shortly before the poem was published, the arrival and rapid intoxication of the guests is conveyed with intermixed shafts of delighted sense and comic satire. 'Soft went the music' (see further discussion of the final version of the passage, p. 145) is repeated. The 'edged Parterres of white bedded snow' are

> Adorne'd along the sides with living flowers
> Conversing, laughing after sunny showers:
>
> (Allott, 643)

but at once we are in a scene like a cartoon one drawn by Gillray or Cruikshank:

> A Glutton drains a cup of Helicon,
> Too fast down, down his throat the brief delight is gone.
> 'Where is that Music?' cries a Lady fair.
> 'Aye, where is it my dear? Up in the air?'
>
> (Allott, 644)

Happily, Keats fastidiously subdued this impulse of excess, and we have instead the comment that drinking accustoms the wondering guests to their surroundings and the events in them, while the restrained summary statement about their intoxication runs:

> Soon was God Bacchus at meridian height;
> Flushed were their cheeks, and bright eyes double bright.
>
> (II, 213–14)

Each participant selects an appropriate garland as he lies 'silk-pillowed at his ease', and Keats gives his three protagonists deeply symbolic ones. Lamia adopts 'the leaves of willow and of adder's tongue', which are emblems of grief and sorrow (Allott, 645); Lycius strips the thyrsus (Bacchus's staff) of its ivy and vine-leaves, perhaps hoping for drunken forgetfulness; and Apollonius dons 'spear-grass and the spiteful thistle' which 'wage/War on his temples'. Those last hostile growths represent the attitude of Apollonius to the folly of his student, and warn of the imminent destruction of the lovers' bliss; they also warn, by inference, that the philosopher, with his scientific thinking and good morality, is superior to the poet, with his intensity of passion and his indulgence in dream. The spear-grass and thistles are there for every poet who is tempted to develop his dream in defiance of reality.

In the key passage which is prelude to the final action, Keats appears grudgingly to accept that the 'consequitive reasoning' (*Letters*, 37) he had distrusted as an adjunct of the creative process has power after all. That the argument about the effect of science on poetry and all things magical and beautiful, including, for instance, the rainbow, is used here, shows Keats engaging, at the onset of his poem's climax, in a current Romantic debate. Allott (645) quotes a lecture given in 1818 by Hazlitt, who had replaced Leigh Hunt as Keats's philosophic and aesthetic mentor, in which Hazlitt observed: 'It cannot be concealed . . . that the progress of knowledge and refinement has a tendency to circumscribe the limits of the imagination, and to clip the wings of poetry.' Keats's agreement with this idea now appears, even though the beauty to be challenged has been described from the first as unreal magic:

> . . . Do not all charms fly
> At the mere touch of cold philosophy?
> There was an awful rainbow once in heaven:
> We know her woof, her texture; she is given
> In the dull catalogue of common things.
> Philosophy will clip an angel's wings,

> Conquer all mysteries by rule and line,
> Empty the haunted air and gnomèd mine –
> Unweave a rainbow, as it erewhile made
> The tender-personed Lamia melt into a shade.
>
> (II, 229–38)

So at this point, Apollonius with his power of truth is presented as destroying something beautiful and gentle, 'the tender-personed Lamia'. His triumph is desolate, creates terror among the guests, and is resisted till the last moment by a Lycius who, watching his heaven dissolve, inveighs against his teacher in a paroxysm of abuse. The only fixed and steady thing in the last scene is the killing glare of Apollonius, which is unpleasant truth in action. It must have been hard for Keats to allow the destruction of the beautiful sensuous dream, and harder still to make Lycius die since, in the Burton source, there is no mention of the young philosopher who marries a lamia forfeiting his life for his moral and aesthetic error.

The final action begins with Lycius, anxious to appease his teacher, tearing his lovelorn eyes from contemplation of Lamia, and looking at Apollonius in hope of pledging him. But the sage has his eyes fixed 'Full on the alarmèd beauty of the bride' and does not respond. Lycius feels her hand, and find it icy. In Burton the lamia pleads with the philosopher, but in Keats her disintegration continues without pause from this moment, and her only plea to Apollonius is a weak hand signal made much later, as she breathes her 'death-breath'. Almost at once, as Lycius looks into her eyes: 'There was no recognition in those orbs'. His loud cry of 'Lamia!' hushes the revelry and stops 'the stately music', and even the ornamental plants start to die:

> The myrtle sickened in a thousand wreaths.
> By faint degrees, voice, lute, and pleasure ceased . . .
>
> (II, 264–5)

> And not a man but felt the terror in his hair.
>
> (II, 268)

Looking at Lamia, Lycius sees that all is blight:

> Lamia, no longer fair, there sat a deathly white.
>
> (II, 276)

And he turns to curse Apollonius, the clear cause, calling down on him 'the righteous ban/Of all the Gods' (278–9) and accusing him of 'impious proud-heart sophistries,/Unlawful magic and enticing lies'

(285–6). This is the only reference in the poem to the magical power of Apollonius, which is mentioned in the classical dictionaries but not by Burton. The shrieks of Lycius are answered by a monosyllable uttered 'in an undertone': 'Fool!' And as Apollonius glares Lamia into annihilation, and twice names her as a serpent, the sage justifies his action to his pupil:

> . . . 'From every ill
> Of life have I preserved thee to this day,
> And shall I see thee made a serpent's prey?
> (II, 296–8)

It is a conclusive justification, and goes some way to put into a reasonable perspective the interruption of Lycius's blisses, as well as the agonized return to serpenthood of Lamia, which is assumed to be her fate. But the death of Lycius is a severe event. In considering the final meaning and emotional close of the poem, it may be best to avoid the question of where the sympathies of the reader are supposed to lie, and instead to accept that *Lamia* presents a conflict in the mind of the poet, a conflict which is not resolved but left in uneasy stasis. The tensions in this stasis have been an almost permanent feature of his poetry from the beginning, and it is hard to think of a major poem by Keats which is without them. Perhaps 'To Autumn' is the only one.

8. *The Fall of Hyperion. A Dream*

Keats's second attempt on the theme of the fall of Hyperion occupied a bare two months, from July to September 1819, though he revised it later. The first canto – and it is significant that he uses the Dantean division 'canto' rather than the Miltonic 'book' – is of 468 lines, the first 293 of which are new, while the rest, beginning 'Deep in the shady sadness of a vale', take up the narrative at the point where *Hyperion* began. The poem then treats the same material as the earlier work, but in a different way, until the end of Canto I, and continues thus until it breaks off at line 61 of Canto II. Keats gave up when describing the arrival of Hyperion, as seen by himself and Moneta, a moment which is reached in *Hyperion* at the end of Book II. So Keats's conviction that his attempt to avoid Miltonics was failing came sooner the second time round.

The difference in mode between the two poems is important. *Hyperion* is structured and presented as an epic, which the poet composes as the detached narrator of a heroic story of universal significance. It is universal in that it proposes an improved dispensation for the gods, and hence for humanity at large. *The Fall of Hyperion. A Dream* offers a personal and virtually purgatorial narrative, in which the events of the former poem are presented imaginatively through two minds: that of the poet-narrator who learns as he suffers, and that of the goddess of memory, Mnemosyne, who is usually called Moneta in this poem. Being the last of the Titans, she suffers as she engages with, and remembers, the defeat of her own dynasty. The details of the fate of the fallen divinities seem therefore not to be related for their own sake, or to inform the world about them in the words of the poet, but rather to be the symbolical background against which Moneta tests the worthiness of the poet John Keats, by bearing on him with all the weight of her penetrating wisdom, her suffering and her holy judgement. It is Moneta's favourable judgement of him that prompts her to allow him to witness, through her revealed memories, the fall of the Titans, which would have led, if the poem had proceeded farther, to the ensuing triumph of Apollo. If *Sleep and Poetry* (December 1816) is an optimistic opening dedication to the chosen art of an exuberant young poet, *The Fall of Hyperion. A Dream*, composed less than three years later, is a mature and agonized interim self-assessment by the same poet.

All three books of *Hyperion* begin with strictly narrative instigations; so it is of special interest that *The Fall of Hyperion* begins with an induction of eighteen lines. The classical epic poet's method of opening a poem or canto was to invoke the muse of epic poetry, Calliope, to enlist her inspiration. Milton naturally invoked the 'Heavenly Muse' of the Holy Spirit. But, with typical originality, Keats uses his induction to advance his hope of posthumous fame; and, in so doing, claims the superiority of poetry over the formal structures offered by religious fanatics and the instinctive spirituality of primitive savages. He regrets that neither avail themselves of the 'melodious utterance' of verse, 'But bare of laurel they live, dream, and die'. Keats insists that they need not be without poetry, and reiterates the view he had expressed long before, in a letter to his fellow-poet J. H. Reynolds in February 1818. This is that every man has the innate capacity of the spider to 'spin from his own inwards his own airy Citadel', that is, to create poetry from his own resources; and if all did so, 'Humanity instead of being a wide heath of Furse and Briars with here and there a remote Oak or Pine, would become a grand democracy of Forest Trees' (*Letters*, 66). In that democracy Keats hopes to be found:

> Whether the dream now purposed to rehearse
> Be poet's or fanatic's will be known
> When this warm scribe my hand is in the grave.
>
> (I, 16–18)

The 'Dream' starts with the poet finding himself in a lush forest landscape, where the sounds of fountains 'soft-showering' and 'the touch/Of scent, not far from roses' suffuses his willing senses. The remains of a banquet, husks, shells and 'grape-stalks but half bare', lie before him, and in the midst 'Stood a cool vessel of transparent juice' (42). It is the world of some of his earlier poems, of *Endymion*, of 'Fancy' and of the 'Ode to Psyche', indulgence in which, symbolized by his gorging the remnants of the feast, makes him thirsty. He drinks from the cool vessel. It contains the drug which will launch his newly entranced poetic sensibility on its purgatorial quest, and when he awakes from 'the cloudy swoon' into which it sent him, the lush vegetation, with its sights, sounds and scents, which had all seemed tangible in their power over him, has disappeared.

A colossal temple wall rears before him. Its size, age and permanence are rendered in Keats's best hyperbolical style:

> I looked around upon the carvèd sides
> Of an old sanctuary with roof august,
> Builded so high it seemed that filmèd clouds
> Might spread beneath, as o'er the stars of heaven.
> So old the place was, I remembered none
> The like upon the earth: what I had seen
> Of grey cathedrals, buttressed walls, rent towers,
> The superannuations of sunk realms,
> Or nature's rocks toiled hard in waves and winds,
> Seemed but the faulture of decrepit things
> To that eternal domèd monument.
>
> (I, 61–71)

For his contrasts Keats draws upon his vividly remembered impressions of the cathedrals in Chichester and Winchester, and the rocky cliffs and caves of Scotland's west coast.

Around him are heaped the tokens of remotely ancient classical religious ceremonies, and under 'the embossèd roof', to the eastward, are huge black gates 'shut against the sunrise evermore'. But to the west he sees

> An Image, huge of feature as a cloud,
> At level of whose feet an altar slept,
>
> (I, 88–9)

and to this altar he moves with awe-struck circumspection. There he becomes aware of a ministrant, whose sacrificial fires fill him with the scents of bliss, to the exclusion of everything else. Then from the 'white fragrant curtains' of 'soft smoke' a voice threatens him:

> . . . 'If thou canst not ascend
> These steps, die on that marble when thou art . . .
>
> (I, 107–8)

> And no hand in the universe can turn
> Thy hourglass if these gummèd leaves be burnt
> Ere thou canst mount up these immortal steps.'
>
> (I, 115–17)

The poet feels 'a palsied chill' strike through his limbs as he struggles against the numbness of death. But he just manages to win:

> Slow, heavy, deadly was my pace; the cold
> Grew stifling, suffocating, at the heart;

> And when I clasped my hands I felt them not.
> One minute before death, my iced foot touched
> The lowest stair; and as it touched, life seemed
> To pour in at the toes. I mounted up,
> As once fair Angels on a ladder flew
> From the green turf to Heaven.
>
> (I, 129–36)

He asks why his life has been spared, and the answer is that since he has learned what it is to suffer and to feel death before his time, his life, and the illumination that continued life will bring, are to be extended. Like most facets of the poem, this must be interpreted symbolically: 'life' represents enhanced poetic achievement. The next utterance of the mysterious figure, whose identity has not yet been disclosed, gives distinctive form to one of Keats's most valued beliefs, and contains a key statement for the understanding of his later poetry:

> 'None can usurp this height,' returned that shade,
> 'But those to whom the miseries of the world
> Are misery, and will not let them rest.
> All else who find a haven in the world,
> Where they may thoughtless sleep away their days,
> If by a chance into this fane they come,
> Rot on the pavement where thou rotted'st half.'
>
> (I, 147–53)

The voice elaborates, and the qualifications it utters warn the poet that, because he is there alone, unaccompanied by the many others who might, like him, 'feel the giant agony of the world', he is 'a dreaming thing'. That is, he aspires to visionary experience, which he will use as a poet, whereas people who know the world's miseries, but are without that yearning, are better than he simply because they are not dreamers.

> They seek no wonder but the human face;
> No music but a happy-noted voice –
> They come not here, they have no thought to come.
>
> (I, 163–5)

The distinction between such dreamers as the poet and all other human beings is made even clearer, and the owner of the voice says it is her understanding of the special difficulty of the dreamer that makes her spare his life, so that he may stand 'safe beneath this statue's knees':

> ... Every creature hath its home;
> Every sole man hath days of joy and pain,
> Whether his labours be sublime or low –
> The pain alone; the joy alone; distinct:
> Only the dreamer venoms all his days,
> Bearing more woe than all his sins deserve.
>
> (I, 171–6)

Accepting with joy that he is 'favoured for unworthiness', he nevertheless defends the poet as 'a sage/A humanist, physician to all men', but modestly does not claim to be one himself. The tall, veiled shape presses him:

> ... 'Art thou not of the dreamer tribe?
> The poet and the dreamer are distinct,
> Diverse, sheer opposite, antipodes.
> The one pours out a balm upon the world,
> The other vexes it.'
>
> (I, 198–202)

For answer, the poet instinctively calls upon Apollo, the god of poetry, to explain why he has used his other divine power, over diseases, to allow bad poetry to be written by

> ... mock lyrists, large self-worshippers
> And careless hectorers in proud bad verse.
>
> (I, 207–8)

The self-worshipper Keats probably had in mind was Wordsworth, with his 'egotistical sublime', and one careless hecterer might well be Byron, whom, after an initial period of adulation, he continuously attacked for his flippancy and cynicism. But the charge against himself is too hurtful to be left in the air, and he positively demands of his interlocutor 'of accent feminine, so courteous' where he is, whose is the altar, and who she is. Her reply introduces the material and theme of the former poem, *Hyperion*:

> '... this old image here,
> Whose carvèd features wrinkled as he fell,
> Is Saturn's; I, Moneta, left supreme,
> Sole priestess of his desolation.'
>
> (I, 224–7)

She is moved, on account of his 'good will' – which I take to be clear from his outburst to Apollo against bad poetry – to reveal to him the scenes of the fall of the Titans, which, she says, are

> Still swooning vivid through my globèd brain,
> With an electral changing misery,
>
> (I, 245–6)

Her agreement to do this is doubly significant. Firstly, it means that she has tacitly accepted his defence of poetry, in which he has clearly defined 'a conception of the true poet . . . as consciously social' (Butler, 152); and that therefore he is not a dreamer who leads a visionary life with his back turned on common humanity. Secondly, it involves the poet in both the fate of the Titans, which is powerlessness and hellish suffering, and the potential achievement of their successor, Apollo. The moment is one in which he faces the terror of death, as Moneta prepares to express her immortal grief:

> As near as an immortal's spherèd words
> Could to a mother's soften, were these last.
> But yet I had a terror of her robes,
> And chiefly of the veils, that from her brow
> Hung pale, and curtained her in mysteries,
> That made my heart too small to hold its blood.
> This saw that Goddess, and with sacred hand
> Parted the veils . . .
>
> (I, 249–56)

This is the last instance in Keats's work of a meeting between a poetic persona of his and a female immortal, and in it the sexually desirable and eternally youthful goddess of previous poems gives way to a mother figure – one whose eternity of suffering is an impersonal grief beyond passion. (A parallel change is in the nature of the moon; it is no longer an active inspirer of love and poetic dreams but a passive, universal comforter.) It is a development of profound significance. The description of Moneta's face, which has been partly quoted when it was compared with the description of the grief-stricken Niobe in *Endymion* (see pp. 27–8), should be dwelled upon as exhibiting Keats operating at his highest level of art on the concept which he regarded as most essential to that art – the necessity and beauty of true suffering exercised in a social frame:

> . . . Then saw I a wan face,
> Not pined by human sorrows, but bright-blanched
> By an immortal sickness which kills not.
> It works a constant change, which happy death
> Can put no end to: deathwards progressing

> To no death was that visage; it had passed
> The lily and the snow; and beyond these
> I must not think now, though I saw that face –
> But for her eyes I should have fled away.
> They held me back, with a benignant light,
> Soft-mitigated by divinest lids
> Half-closed, and visionless entire they seemed
> Of all external things – they saw me not,
> But in bland splendour beamed like the mild moon,
> Who comforts those she sees not, who knows not
> What eyes are upward cast . . .
>
> (I, 256–71)

The moment brings the old poem and the new into joint focus. In response to the narrator's adoring demand to know 'what high tragedy/ In the dark secret chambers of her skull/Was acting', Moneta begins to show the substance of her grief, with the reiteration of the well-remembered opening of *Hyperion*:

> Deep in the shady sadness of a vale,
> Far sunken from the healthy breath of morn,
> Far from the fiery noon and eve's one star.
>
> (I, 294–6)

Moneta points out to him the features of her world of memory, taking on the function of a Dantean guide. It is one of several respects in which Keats shows that Dante has largely replaced Milton as his poetic mentor. As Virgil and Beatrice guided Dante through hell, purgatory and heaven, so Moneta guides the poet through a classical purgatory. Here she reveals the fallen divinity of Saturn; not long afterwards she identifies Thea, Hyperion's wife, as she approaches (332), and at the end of Canto I she explains that Saturn and Thea, when they leave, 'Are speeding to the families of grief' (i.e., the defeated Titans, 461). Finally, she is the expositor of all but the last dozen lines of the short second canto, in which she describes Hyperion aching with the horrors of his coming collapse.

Keats's reworking of the material of the first two books of *Hyperion* is highly conscious, as he aims at precise effects. The first effect has already been mentioned: it is to weaken the Miltonic epic quality of the earlier poem by presenting the fall of the pre-Olympians through the mind of the suffering Titaness Moneta, to whose memory the poet-narrator deservedly wins access. By his participation in her grief he becomes not only a fellow-sufferer of hers but a poet to whom the agonies of the Titans represent 'the miseries of the world'. Those agonies are thus felt almost internally by the poet and are expressed in the narration, whether by Moneta or himself, with emphasis on his emotional experience, and his interpretation of that experience. There is a wonderful moment when this process is suddenly drawn together in a single image: after the arrival of Thea at Saturn's side, the poet sees them together, with Moneta, as 'three fixèd shapes':

> . . . Without stay or prop
> But my own weak mortality, I bore
> The load of this eternal quietude,
> The unchanging gloom, and the three fixèd shapes
> Ponderous upon my senses a whole moon.
> For by my burning brain I measured sure
> Her silver seasons shedded on the night,
> And ever day by day methought I grew
> More gaunt and ghostly. Oftentimes I prayed
> Intense, that death would take me from the vale
> And all its burthens . . .
>
> (I, 388–98)

The epic descriptions and heroic similes are much reduced, some being altogether excluded and some being diminished in pictorial effect. Among the sections in *Hyperion* which are rejected are the Miltonic catalogue describing the fallen Titans, and their debate on whether to accept their fate or to strive to regain their former eminence. Both had clearly been inspired by Books I and II of *Paradise Lost*, and could have been abandoned on that ground alone, but to retain them would have meant placing less emphasis on the suffering involved in the defeat of the Titans. Similarly, Saturn's attitude to his fall is changed. In *Hyperion* he makes a long speech of defiance to his peers, which clearly owes much to Satan's tremendous speeches in those two books of *Paradise Lost*. In *The Fall of Hyperion* Saturn's defiance is immeasurably enfeebled, so that in the twenty-seven lines he speaks, lamentation is uppermost, with the word 'moan' occurring twelve times; while his call to arms is so permeated with sheer weakness as to lack credibility altogether:

> Oh, oh, the pain, the pain of feebleness.
> Moan, moan, for still I thaw – or give me help:
> Throw down those imps, and give me victory.
>
> (I, 429–31)

Not surprisingly, Moneta, in reporting the departure of Saturn and Thea 'to the families of grief', says that the Titans have 'no hope'. That is in direct contrast to their state of mind in *Hyperion*, where Thea finds that Saturn's speech of defiance

> '. . . cheers our fallen house. Come to our friends,
> O Saturn! come away, and give them heart! . . .'
>
> (I, 150–51)

In the new poem the presentation of Hyperion as a superior and dazzling god, the resident of a majestic palace in heaven, is deliberately toned down and shortened; and, although some of the lines of the former poem are kept, their effect is different because they are spoken in sorrow by Moneta instead of being uttered by the voice of the epic poet. Yet, significantly, it was at this point in the narration, with Moneta having guided the poet to Hyperion's palace, that Keats abandoned the poem.

The best way fully to register and understand all the differences which have been discussed in Keats's two treatments of what is ostensibly the same theme is to make a detailed comparison of parallel sections. The arrival of Thea at Saturn's side, their exchanges and departure to meet their fellows in defeat, as treated in the two poems, suggests itself: *Hyperion*, I, 22–157 and *The Fall of Hyperion. A Dream*, I, 327–468. About fifty of the lines are the same, or the same with the exception of a changed word or two, but the essential meaning of the later poem is different, and the tone is more concentrated upon expression of a sorrow which cannot be alleviated. In addition the presence of two sorrowing goddesses, Thea and Moneta, together with the radical curtailment of Saturn's role, work so as to suffuse the new poem with a strongly feminine spirit of compassion and power to suffer. That spirit and that power, Keats aspires to absorb as essential to the fulfilment of his poetic destiny. It seems to me that in the poem before us, he unwittingly achieved his poetic purpose before completing the narrative which he had planned to sustain it: and that may be the main reason why he did not proceed. Moneta does for him what he intended Hyperion to do.

Whether the poem is felt to be complete or not, it stands as a moving and beautifully precise debate about what it is to be the poet John Keats, and in this respect it is more informative than, and as passionate as, the Spring Odes of 1819. The concept of 'poet', beginning with apparently solipsistic preoccupations, steadily reaches out into concerns which for nearly two hundred years have remained central to modern art in all its forms. The self-doubt of the artist is one of the most productive of these concerns. If the artist is special because he possesses unusual insights and other gifts, is he therefore by nature, or by conviction, or by reason of being rejected, separate from society?

The artist must, in the words of Conrad's butterfly-collector Stein, in that ironically entitled novel *Lord Jim*, 'in the destructive element immerse'; must, that is, pursue his dream despite the personal and social consequences. But it is the truly Romantic, and subsequently modern, attitude that such immersion should be continuously questioned and evaluated afresh, in the light of humane criteria. As he immerses himself, the poet must share the burdens and miseries of common humanity, in order to align himself with forces which work for a better world. In *The Fall of Hyperion. A Dream* the aesthetics of poetry and political idealism mingle and reinforce each other.

9. Dramatic Attempts and the Last Shorter Poems

In this final chapter of a chronological study of Keats's poetic output, it remains to consider what he wrote during his last year of creative work, leaving aside the two major narrative poems, *Lamia* and *The Fall of Hyperion. A Dream*, which are the subjects of the two preceding chapters. The work before us consists of two dramatic pieces, the one complete play, *Otho the Great*, and nearly two hundred lines of Act I of *King Stephen*, both of which were composed in the second half of 1819; two well-known lyrics, the sonnet 'Bright Star' and the ode-like poem of three stanzas, 'To Autumn', which have been dated to the autumn of 1819, the latter to the third week in September; the 'comic faery poem in the Spenser stanza', as Brown described *The Cap and Bells; or, The Jealousies*, which is an unfinished poem of almost eight hundred lines, also written during the autumn and early days of winter; and a handful of poems addressed to Fanny Brawne, including two sonnets and an ode, which were written between the time of his reunion with her early in October, after a separation of nearly four months, and the time in February 1820 just after he had had the lung haemorrhage which he knew indicated that he was fatally ill. There are also one or two fragments and light pieces.

The Plays

Otho the Great and *King Stephen* are the only products of Keats's intention concerning his writing, stated to Taylor in November 1819, to make his 'chief Attempt in the Drama'. He always meant, and indeed expected, somewhat airily, to compose 'a few fine plays'. His lifelong admiration of Shakespeare had early led him to the London theatre, where, while writing reviews for such papers as the *Champion*, he paid tribute to the acting of Edmund Kean. It was of Kean that Hazlitt wrote that watching him act was 'like reading Shakespeare by flashes of lightning'. Keats felt a strong affinity with the actor, who was, like himself, short and capable of expressing great intensity in his art. Kean performed in what was called 'legitimate drama', that is to say, plays licensed by the Lord Chamberlain, who had jurisdiction within a twenty-mile radius of Westminster, and such plays, which included those by Shakespeare, could be performed only at the two patent theatres, Drury Lane and Covent Garden.

Both these theatres were huge, and were constantly being enlarged by managers eager to house even bigger audiences. They could take three thousand. Admission was to the theatre, not to a particular seat; so people who got in then manoeuvred or fought or paid to get a place with a good view of the stage. The auditorium was lit throughout the performance, and people were admitted, and could leave, at any time. Various kinds of wick and oil lamps illuminated the place, with concentration on the acting area, before the arrival of gas lighting at Drury Lane during the year in which Keats wrote *Endymion*, 1817. During Keats's adolescence both these enormous places were burnt to the ground and then rebuilt.

In such theatres most of the audience were far from the stage and so unable to hear the spoken word unless it was bellowed; so the patent houses became, as one dramatist put it, 'theatres for spectators rather than playhouses for hearers'. Spectacle, including lavish display and scenic transformation, became the obvious resort of theatre managers; and in these respects English stagecraft and mechanics were considerably ahead of continental theatres.

This was the kind of theatre for which Keats, like other Romantic poets, presumed to write plays in emulation of Shakespeare. Wordsworth wrote *The Borderers*; Coleridge collaborated with Southey in *The Fall of Robespierre* and produced *Osirio* on his own; Shelley's play was *The Cenci*, which he did not expect to receive public presentation, since its main subject was incest; and Byron, who was for a time on the board of management of Drury Lane, wrote several plays, before expressing contempt for the debased stage of the time and branching out into a new kind of verse drama analogous to the epic drama of Goethe, to whom he dedicated two plays. Shelley called his *Prometheus Unbound* a 'lyric drama', which places it in the category of Goethe's *Faust*. But Shakespeare was the dominant influence on all.

OTHO THE GREAT

Mundane as well as artistic considerations led Keats to the actual writing of a play. During the summer of 1819 he had become discouraged at his failure to publish poetry profitably, and almost in despair had talked of going to sea as a ship's doctor in order to earn enough money to marry Fanny. His friend Brown, horrified, suggested that in collaboration he and Keats should write a tragedy for performance at

Drury Lane. Brown had already had a musical play staged and, presuming on his greater experience of the drama, undertook to supply a plot and characters, act by act, which Keats would versify with appropriate characterization, though without knowing the detail of what was to happen in the following act. This arrangement was proceeded with up to the end of Act IV, at which point Keats objected to the melodramatic complication of the proposed denouement and worked alone on Act V. Following the fashion of the day, in which the plays of Goethe and Schiller in translation figured, they took a historical German subject, *Otho the Great*, a tenth-century monarch who became Holy Roman Emperor.

The main details of the plot are as follows. Otho forgives his son, Ludolph, for intriguing against him, and arranges to marry him to Auranthe, the unchaste sister of the villainous Conrad, Duke of Franconia. These two have slandered the chaste Erminia so that she is no longer the chosen affianced of Ludolph. Albert, the former lover of Auranthe, discovers their plots and, after killing Conrad, dies of his wounds. Ludolph goes mad and dies heart-broken when he is told the truth by a priest. That summary does not register the many twists and turns of the intrigue, or such fancy theatrical circumstances as that in which Ludolph disguises himself as an Arab warrior to fight against his father's enemies, and then quixotically tries to conceal the fact from his magnanimous parent.

Besides the blank verse, other factors of poetics and plot constantly remind readers that Keats takes the Elizabethan and Jacobean theatres as models, with Shakespeare chiefly, but also such dramatists as Webster and Marlowe, often in mind. For example, the play opens with the villain, Conrad, declaring himself to the audience in a soliloquy, rather like Richard III. Then, Erminia is traduced by a trumped-up story about a man at her window at night, like that by which Hero, in *Much Ado About Nothing*, is traduced. And there is an honest father-figure, the priest Ethelbert, who defends the chaste and the true, and is at first not believed.

The part of Ludolph was written with Kean in mind. He was the only actor Keats thought capable of playing it. Soon after Keats started on *King Stephen*, Kean left for America; and then Drury Lane, after at first accepting the play for performance, declined to proceed, a refusal which was followed by a peremptory rejection by Covent Garden. Subsequently, Keats abruptly stopped writing plays.

It is worth looking at two examples of the quality of Keats's dramatic writing in *Otho*, one of them for his treatment of dramatic situation, and the other for the application of his poetic gift to the drama. For the first, the initial entry of the character intended to be acted by Kean, Otho's son and heir, Ludolph, is as important as any. It takes place at the beginning of the third scene of the play, and is therefore well on in the exposition. The first scene has introduced the villain and his sister, as well as Albert, who is to expose them. The second features Otho, magnanimous in victory, freeing a captured enemy prince and yearning for reconciliation with his son; this scene 'closes' (a stage direction which reminds us that the nineteenth-century English theatre had forgotten all about the practice of 'scene unlimited' in Shakespeare's theatre, which allowed the action to continue without a break even when the notional locale changed) with the holy Ethelbert 'and six monks' musically blessing the magnanimous monarch. Hard upon this spectacular event, Ludolph enters with his confidant Sigifred, who in conversation describes and marvels at Ludolph's battle achievements as an Arab, at his humility in not expecting his father's forgiveness, at his unbridled love for that same father, and at his proud reluctance to sue for forgiveness. Disguise, humility, filial love and noble pride are drawn from the heroic drama's stock of theatrical clichés, and the spectacle of their display is rounded off by the hero's confession of love for Auranthe, whom, at this stage as far as Ludolph knows, he is forbidden by Otho to marry:

> I will encounter his thwart spleen myself
> To-day, at the Duke Conrad's, where he keeps
> His crowded state after the victory.
> There will I be, a most unwelcome guest,
> And parley with him, as a son should do
> Who doubly loathes a father's tyranny;
>
> (I, iii, 91–6)

> Aye, and those turreted Franconian walls,
> Like to a jealous casket, hold my pearl –
> My fair Auranthe! Yes, I will be there.
>
> (I, iii, 102–4)

The scene ends with Ludolph being summoned to the royal presence; the demands of suspense have been met, because we have been sympathetically given the subject, but not the outcome, of the meeting which is to follow. Fair dramaturgy, run-of-the-mill popular dramatic verse.

The last act which, as has been noted, is Keats's own, gave the poet particular satisfaction, and in despite of some critics, I think I can see why. It certainly contains the best dramatic verse in the play, and although the culminating situations are extremely theatrical, they are logical consequences of preceding actions, with the possible exception of the last piece of the action. The climax is that Ludolph goes mad and dies at his wedding banquet because he has been deceived by Auranthe, who frustrates his desire for revenge by stabbing herself to death off-stage. Ample quotation from this richly public melodramatic scene is really required to make my point, but perhaps some idea of the dramatic verse may be gained from the following passage. As Ludolph feels madness coming on, he dresses his circumstance in magnificence:

> I would have, as a mortal I may not,
> Hangings of heaven's clouds, purple and gold,
> Slung from the spheres; gauzes of silver mist,
> Looped up with cords of twisted wreathèd light,
> And tasselled round with weeping meteors!
> These pendent lamps and chandeliers are bright
> As earthly fires from dull dross can be cleansed;
> Yet could my eyes drink up intenser beams
> Undazzled – this is darkness! When I close
> These lids, I see far fiercer brilliances –
> Skies full of splendid moons, and shooting stars,
> And spouting exhalations, diamond fires,
> And panting fountains quivering with deep glows!
> Yes – this is dark – is it not dark?
>
> (V, v, 35–48)

And like a Shakespearean hero, dying to music as Henry IV did, he speaks his own epitaph of self-justification – though it may be observed that he exhibits no tragic fault apart from believing Erminia to be good and Auranthe to be bad:

> . . . A fine-spun vengeance!
> Carve it on my tomb, that when I rest beneath
> Men shall confess – This Prince was gulled and cheated,
> But from the ashes of disgrace he rose
> More than a fiery dragon, and did burn
> His ignominy up in purging fires!
> Did I not send, sir, but a moment past,
> For my father?
>
> (V, v, 129–36)

It is a Coriolanus-like moment, topped off by melodramatic filial yearning.

116

Perhaps Keats was satisfied with his work on the ending of *Otho* because he identified so strongly with the hero as well as with the actor who was meant to play the part, and also worked off some of his own preoccupations with love and death. The conflict between injured innocence, as represented by Erminia, and evil unchastity, as represented by Auranthe, takes place in the mind of Ludolph, who may be perceived, like other Keats heroes, as a type of the poet. The two women express different aspects of Keats's varying perceptions of Fanny Brawne. Ward (308) notes the extraordinary parallels between the endings of *Otho the Great* and *Lamia*, the poem which Keats rounded off in a rush a few days after completing the play: 'In both the play and the poem there is a father-figure who tries to win the infatuated lover back to the truth; in both the woman deceives her lover and is punished by death; and in both the man dies on his wedding-night, broken-hearted at the exposure of his bride's falsity.'

KING STEPHEN

To move from the Gothic hothouse of *Otho* to the English battlefield of the first three scenes of *King Stephen* is to enter a new theatrical world. The valour and defiance in defeat of Stephen at the battle of Lincoln in 1141 are celebrated in muscular verse replete with correct historical terms, and there is no echo anywhere in the surviving text of Keats's personal preoccupations, which are so evident in *Otho* and *Lamia*. Here is the Second Knight describing Stephen at bay after his army has lost the battle:

> He shames our victory. His valour still
> Keeps elbow-room amid our eager swords,
> And holds our bladed falchions all aloof –
> His gleaming battle-axe being slaughter-sick,
> Smote on the morion of a Flemish knight,
> Broke short in his hand; upon the which he flung
> The heft away with such a vengeful force,
> It paunched the Earl of Chester's horse, who then
> Spleen-hearted came in full career at him.
>
> (I, ii, 35–43)

The unfinished fourth scene takes place in the Presence Chamber of the Empress Maud, whose army under the Earl of Gloucester has defeated Stephen. The business of the scene is the vengeful lady's objections to the chivalrous treatment of her captured enemy by Gloucester.

In Keats's dramatic verse her characterization is as forceful as that of
Stephen, and poetic compression and vividness are present in all the
dialogue. The last few lines consist of the Earl of Chester's account of
Gloucester's hosting of the prisoner, after Maud has sent for Gloucester:

> *Chester.*   And for his perjury,
> Gloucester has fit rewards – nay, I believe,
> He sets his bustling household's wits at work
> For flatteries to ease this Stephen's hours,
> And make a heaven of his purgatory;
> Adorning bondage with the pleasant gloss
> Of feasts and music, and all idle shows
> Of indoor pageantry; while siren whispers
> Predestined for his ear, 'scape as half-checked
> From lips the courtliest and the rubiest
> Of all the realm, admiring of his deeds.
> *Maud.*   A frost upon his summer!
> *Chester.*   A queen's nod
> Can make his June December. Here he comes . . .
>
> (I, iv, 46–58)

From Colvin and De Selincourt onwards, critics have admiringly
compared the battle scenes with those in the English chronicle plays of
Shakespeare. Whether one responds with delight or cautious sympathy
to a good pastiche of a dramatic idiom two hundred years old may be a
matter of personal taste. But I do perceive a real difference, which may
be obscured by the fact that Keats's use of blank verse is quite like
Shakespeare's. The latter's battle scenes are conducted with Renaissance
weapons, insofar as the detail is relevant to the dramatic discourse
being pursued; Keats's display a deliberate historicism, as perusal of
even the Second Knight's short speech will make clear. In writing the
play, Keats was as accurately faithful to the Romantic period's medieval
inspiration as any poet, and *King Stephen* could be classified as a
'medieval' play in the making in just the same way as *The Eve of St
Agnes*, 'La Belle Dame Sans Merci' and *Isabella* have been classified as
'medieval' love stories. The spirit of the age of chivalry is in those four
scenes.

Fanny Brawne Poems

Of these five poems, three belong with virtual certainty to October and

118

November 1819, and express Keats's renewed passion for Fanny after the reunion which followed a separation of about four months. That separation had been enforced by Keats himself during the early summer because he had become so obsessed with her that he felt incapable of concentrating on his writing if she were near by. He went to Shanklin on the Isle of Wight, was soon joined by Brown, and went on to Winchester, where he completed *Otho the Great* before returning to London in early October. During those four months his output was prodigious: besides *Otho*, he composed *Lamia*, *The Fall of Hyperion*, *King Stephen* and 'To Autumn'.

The first of the three poems which celebrate – if that is the word – the reunion of Keats and Fanny is the bemused sonnet, 'The day is gone, and all its sweets are gone!' It is a poem of almost stunned recollection after Fanny has left him one evening. She is the day, the close of which separates her from him in a quadruple fading:

> Faded the flower and all its budded charms,
>   Faded the sight of beauty from my eyes,
> Faded the shape of beauty from my arms,
>   Faded the voice, warmth, whiteness, paradise.
>   (5–8)

In form the sonnet is Shakespearean, with a rather weak ending in which Keats uses the final couplet suddenly to compare his daytime with her with an act of prayer. But before that, the last quatrain expresses his passionate regret that he cannot use the ensuing night for making love to her:

> Vanished unseasonably at shut of eve,
>   When the dusk holiday, or holinight,
> Of fragrant-curtained love begins to weave
>   The woof of darkness thick, for hid delight;
> But, as I've read love's missal through to-day,
> He'll let me sleep, seeing I fast and pray.
>   (9–14)

The next poem, 'To——' (that is, Fanny), describes total fascination, and rebellion against being so dominated:

> What can I do to drive away
> Remembrance from my eyes? For they have seen,
> Ay, an hour ago, my brilliant Queen!
> Touch has a memory. Oh, say, love, say,

> What can I do to kill it and be free
> In my old liberty?
>
> (1–6)

He wishes to be a sea-bird winging free over the sea, as he once was, 'When every fair one that I saw was fair', and he could be 'above/The reach of fluttering Love'. He considers the conventional escape offered by drink, in a style much inferior to the expression of the same idea in 'Ode to a Nightingale', but recognizes that 'wine is only sweet to happy men'. And he is unhappy, suffering 'dismal cares' on account of his brother George's financial failure in America. This brings in Keats's famous diatribe against 'that most hateful land', which he describes in thirteen lines as hostile, infertile and without even such river gods as adorn the land of his beloved Greek mythology. That strange irruption into what began as a love poem over, the poem subsides into a conclusion expressing inchoate longing:

> Oh, let me once more rest
> My soul upon that dazzling breast!
>
> (48–9)

> Oh, the sweetness of the pain!
> Give me those lips again!
> Enough! Enough! It is enough for me
> To dream of thee!
>
> (54–7)

The first line of the third poem, 'I cry your mercy, pity, love', indicates the medieval origin of its thought. Keats, like the courtly lover of old, appeals to his lady's mercy and pity to make her yield:

> . . . in pity give me all,
> Withhold no atom's atom or I die.
>
> (9–10)

The trouble with these three poems is that Keats remains so close to his prime object that enriching imagery and original thought are virtually absent. Perhaps only 'Touch has a memory' stays in the mind: it is a happy example of Keats's many deliberate fusions of different kinds of sense experience.

'Ode to Fanny' was the last poem addressed to her, as far as we know. Almost certainly it belongs to the time immediately after Keats suffered his first lung haemorrhage. It is a strictly autobiographical poem which expresses, besides the state of his mind with its hopes and fears, actual situations. Thus, it opens with a reference to the bleeding he underwent as part of the medical treatment, and when he calls upon Apollo for a poetic theme, there is Fanny, standing in the garden and looking in on him because she is forbidden to come nearer for fear of infection:

> I come – I see thee, as thou standest there,
> Beckon me out into the wintry air.
>
> (7–8)

Most of the rest of the poem expresses fear that, now he is incapable, she will respond to some other man; in his 'torturing jealousy' he sees her at a dance being tempted:

> . . . Though music breathe
> Voluptuous visions into the warm air,
> Though swimming through the dance's dangerous wreath,
> Be like an April day,
> Smiling and cold and gay,
>
> (25–9)

In the fifth stanza he applies to her, without any evidence, conventional distrust of feminine good faith:

> Must not a woman be
> A feather on the sea,
> Swayed to and fro by every wind and tide?
> (36–8)

There is little pleasure in dwelling on such morbid suspicions, which seem to be the product of a sick man's mind. The technical interest of the poem is discussed on p. 147, where the jealous outburst of the final stanza is quoted.

Of the poems addressed to, or about Fanny, the sonnet 'Bright star! Would I were steadfast as thou art' is left. At one time it was thought to have been written on shipboard on the way to Italy, and so was regarded as the last poem Keats wrote; but as Brown firmly dated it 1819, it is now usually regarded as a product of late autumn in that year. Unlike the four poems just considered, it approaches its subject by one of the most resplendent images in the whole work of Keats; the bright star symbolizes the steadfastness he longed for in his relationship with Fanny. The star as an image of permanence is a common one in poetry; everyone is familiar with Shakespeare's 116th sonnet, which celebrates love as 'an ever-fixèd mark':

> It is the star to every wandering bark,
>   Whose worth's unknown, although his height be taken.
>
> (7–8)

Keats, in returning to a concept he had used before, creates a visionary planetary scene observed from the point of view of his star and then, hyperbolically, trumps the eternal steadfastness he has put into the reader's mind with an image of himself pillowed on Fanny's breast:

> Bright star! Would I were steadfast as thou art –
>   Not in lone splendour hung aloft the night
> And watching, with eternal lids apart,
>   Like nature's patient, sleepless eremite,
> The moving waters at their priest-like task
>   Of pure ablution round earth's human shores,
> Or gazing on the new soft-fallen mask
>   Of snow upon the mountains and the moors;
> No – yet still steadfast, still unchangeable,
>   Pillowed upon my fair love's ripening breast,
> To feel for ever its soft fall and swell,
>   Awake for ever in a sweet unrest,
> Still, still to hear her tender-taken breath,
> And so live ever – or else swoon to death.

The image of the octave, with its transcendent and tranquil imaginative effect, cannot be trumped by such a commonplace real picture as that of the sestet, personally specific though resting one's head for ever on the gently heaving breast of one's lover may be. I prefer to stay suspended in space beside the star, looking down on the wintry earth under nature's governance: the trick of the poem goes to the star image.

The Cap and Bells; or, The Jealousies

This poem, some of the circumstances connected with the writing of which are given on p. 146, was composed during November and December 1819. According to Brown, who encouraged him in the venture, Keats spent his mornings working on it fast, with Brown in attendance, copying out each stanza as it was completed. But in the evenings Keats insisted on being alone, and was busy revising *The Fall of Hyperion*. *The Jealousies* was the preferred title of Keats, who proposed to publish the poem pseudonymously, under the name of 'Lucy Vaughan Lloyd of China Walk, Lambeth' (Allott, 701). The main characters of the poem are the Emperor Elfinan and the Princess Bellanaine (= 'pretty dwarf'), both faery persons who have the propensity, alarming to members of their courts, of falling in love with mortals instead of fellow-fairies. However, Elfinan decides to marry Bellanaine, and sends an embassy to fetch her. But as soon as the bridal ambassadors have left, he sends for the magician Hum, to enlist his aid in gaining access to the mortal girl he loves, Bertha (the name of Keats's own heroine of *The Eve of St Mark*). As Bellanaine arrives with her entourage, sorrowfully remembering her mortal lover Hubert, Elfinan, with the magic book of Hum under his arm, salutes her from a distance and disappears, quoting 'Byron's poem to his wife after their separation, "Fare Thee Well"' (Allott, 729):

> He bowed at Bellanaine, and said, 'Poor Bell!
> *Farewell! Farewell! and if for ever, still*
> *For ever fare thee well!'* – and then he fell
> A laughing, snapped his fingers – shame it is to tell.
>
> (609–12)

The rest of the poem is occupied mainly with the account of what the chamberlain Crafticanto, Elfinan's envoy, writes in his diary about the journey back to the Emperor's palace in India with Bellanaine, who proves a petulant charge with whom to while away the journey time:

> She wished a game at whist, made three revokes,
>
> (700)

> She cried for chess – I played a game with her.
>
> (703)

They arrive to be met, not by a welcoming imperial bridegroom, but by a rabble of courtiers panicking at the absence of Elfinan. Crafticanto seeks out Hum, whom he finds 'far gone in liquor'. At the point at which Hum 'Came forth to quell the hubbub in the hall', the poem breaks off. It contains some turgid fancy on obvious subjects, some of them topical, but little wit, as the example in line 700 quoted above indicates.

'To Autumn' and 'This Living Hand Now Warm and Capable'

In treating these two poems last, I ignore the probable order of composition because I want to conclude with poems of rare worth and substance. It daunts me a little to focus afresh on 'To Autumn' which, together with the Spring Odes, several sonnets, *The Eve of St Agnes* and *Hyperion*, has been an essential piece of my spiritual furniture for fifty-five years. I have always been able, without the text in front of me, to relive the experience of the poem and relate it to my own life and the world about me. It is probably best to begin with my deep conviction about the works of literature, music and art that I have liked most. Tranquillity and serenity lie at the heart of the most profound artistic response to life; the great artist has mastered his or her experience of what life has bombarded the soul with: vicissitude and mutability in all their forms – ecstatic joy, tragic loss in love or fortune, change and decay in the individual and in nature. Artistic beauty inheres in the right perception of these and such other things, and the creative raptures and pains which express the perceptions proceed from a centre with a harmonious impulse. It is as true of a poem as of acting that the creator must, as Hamlet advised the Players, in the 'whirlwind' of his 'passion . . . acquire and beget a temperance that may give it a smoothness'.

Such ideas are in harmony with the poetic ideals presented in *The Fall of Hyperion*. 'A poet is a sage,/A humanist, physician to all men', and one of those

> 'Who love their fellows even to the death;
> Who feel the giant agony of the world;
> And more, like slaves to poor humanity,
> Labour for mortal good? . . .'

(I, 156–9)

'To Autumn' is, after all, a valedictory poem. In presenting the rich fruits of dead summer in connection with approaching winter, in harmonizing the productive work of humanity with the autumnal processes of dominant nature, and in recording and projecting all these elements through a surveying consciousness of mind, eye and ear meditatively attuned to the essential melancholy and beauty of the subject, it achieves a richly consolatory farewell.

The structure of the poem is unusual. Although a personified Autumn is addressed throughout, in the first and last of the three stanzas the many related images presented are of actuality, and not metaphorical in any sense. The 'mossed cottage-trees' bent down with apples of the first

stanza, like the 'barrèd clouds' which 'bloom the soft-dying day' of the
last, are precisely real as seen and felt by Keats. But the middle stanza
follows a subtly various personification of Autumn through several
harvest activities; we see this imaginary figure, which seems sometimes
male and sometimes female, all the time we are reading. It is autumnal
nature in human form. This difference between the middle stanza and
the other two, together with the evidence of much correction in the
draft, has led to a general supposition that the poem originally consisted
of just the first and last stanzas, and that the middle one was the
product of a reconsideration of the whole. If that is correct, and I think
it well may be, then it is a demonstration of Keats's acute sense of
design, as well as of his instinct for the perfect completion of an inspired
idea. I can see him with the first and last stanzas fully drafted in front
of him, wondering if he had achieved the perfection of the experience of
his Sunday walk, as he described it in a letter to Reynolds: 'How
beautiful the season is now – How fine the air. A temperate sharpness
about it ... Dian skies – I never lik'd stubble fields so much as now –
Aye better than the chilly green of the spring. Somehow a stubble plain
looks warm ... I composed upon it' (*Letters*, 291–2). He found that
the way to perfect the poem was to emphasize the human as part of
nature, and the second stanza is the result.

The prosodical and, to a limited extent, the linguistic characteristics
of the poem are briefly indicated on p. 143. Here the aim is to follow its
inner process.

It begins with a subdued apostrophe to Autumn; subdued because
the personification goes only as far as suggesting a conspiracy with the
sun to work for ripeness. And for the rest of the first stanza ripeness, as
conveyed chiefly by a succession of powerful and simple verbs, is all.
The vines are *loaded* with fruit, the trees are *bent* by the weight of
apples, gourds are *swelled*, hazel shells *plumped*, and late flowers are
budded for the bees, whose clammy cells are accordingly *o'er-brimmed*.
The concentration on what happens inside small natural growths such
as fruits, nuts and flowers impresses fullness, sweetness and warmth
upon the mind, with an interior sense of nature's plenitude. The human
work of the season, the exterior physical scene, the sky above, are yet
to come:

> Season of mists and mellow fruitfulness,
>   Close bosom friend of the maturing sun,
> Conspiring with him how to load and bless
>   With fruit the vines that round the thatch-eves run:

> To bend with apples the mossed cottage-trees,
>> And fill all fruit with ripeness to the core;
>>> To swell the gourd, and plump the hazel shells
>> With a sweet kernel; to set budding more
> And still more, later flowers for the bees,
> Until they think warm days will never cease,
>> For summer has o'erbrimmed their clammy cells.
>>> (1–11)

The personifications in the second stanza present a mysterious ambiguity, but three of the four figures share one characteristic: a kind of beautiful lethargy, compounded of repletion and ecstatic acceptance of their roles in the fulfilment of the season. Thus the first figure, evidently a woman, is sitting on a granary floor 'careless', her 'hair soft-lifted by the winnowing wind'. Keats is expressing his longstanding love affair with the word 'soft', not just on its own, but as the component of a compound adjective, which is repeated in the 'soft-dying day' of the last stanza. It is a word of harmonious warmth, which occurs twice in 'Bright star!'

The next figure, presumably a male one, is asleep 'on a half-reaped furrow' and 'Drowsed with the fume of poppies', so drugged that he cannot finish the job. The third is the exception to the blissful lethargy; apparently a female, because women and children usually did the gleaning when reaping was completed, she is pictured walking on a bridge across a brook, with her load on her head. And the last figure, which might be of either sex, though I see it as male, is idly watching the oozings from a cyder-press. All are ordinary human beings at their autumn occupations, spellbound and accepting, in a world which has opened out from the succulent insides of the fruits in the first stanza.

> Who hath not seen thee oft amid thy store?
>> Sometimes whoever seeks abroad may find
> Thee sitting careless on a granary floor,
>> Thy hair soft-lifted by the winnowing wind;
> Or on a half-reaped furrow sound asleep,
>> Drowsed with the fume of poppies, while thy hook
>>> Spares the next swath and all its twinèd flowers;
> And sometimes like a gleaner thou dost keep
>> Steady thy laden head across a brook;
>> Or by a cyder-press, with patient look,
>>> Thou watchest the last oozings, hours by hours.
>>> (12–22)

It has been credibly suggested, by Ian Jack (*Keats and the Mirror of Art*, 1967) and others, that 'the pictorial details are probably inspired by various paintings' (Allott, 652), but the concentration on autumnal function in such words as 'granary', 'winnowing', 'swath', 'laden' and 'oozings' keeps working reality in the forefront.

The poem lifts from the serenely swelling and sweetening of the insides of fruits, nuts and flowers in the first stanza, to the human efforts to store the autumnal plenitude made possible by nature in the second stanza. In the third stanza it must lift again, not only to universalize and consolidate these two experiences, but to take the reader into acceptance of autumn's essential farewell, with its suggestion of death. It must do that by uniting the supernal – in the process of time, in the ineluctable change of sky and earth, and in the threat of barrenness in the coming winter – with the natural and physical – in the form of the cropped fields of stubble, the creatures now strong and mature which were born naked and feeble in the spring, the insects whose thriving existence is due to the superabundance of autumnal warmth and food supply, and the birds, some of which, like the robins, will face out the coming winter, and others which, like the swallows, will leave for summery places in huge flocks, to return when winter is gone. Keats's device for this is twofold: he opens out from the local human scene of the second stanza to the natural perimeters of the English rural world, with its skies, clouds, winds, hills and rivers; and he does this largely, but not exclusively, by sound symphonies which complement the visual symphonies of the second stanza.

> Where are the songs of spring? Aye, where are they?
> Think not of them, thou hast thy music too –
> While barrèd clouds bloom the soft-dying day,
> And touch the stubble-plains with rosy hue.
> Then in a wailful choir the small gnats mourn
> Among the river-sallows, borne aloft
> Or sinking, as the light wind lives or dies;
> And full-grown lambs loud bleat from hilly bourn;
> Hedge-crickets sing, and now with treble soft
> The red-breast whistles from a garden-croft,
> And gathering swallows twitter in the skies.
>
> (23–33)

The characteristic Keatsian synaesthesia – the enriching fusion of two or more senses – is there in the first four lines, where the pink reflection of sunlit evening clouds on the stubble-plains, which is of course a visual effect, is called 'music'. To this imagined music is added the down-to-earth music of mourning gnats, big bleating lambs, singing crickets, whistling robins and twittering swallows. To place simple, popular, onomatopoeic words such as 'whistle' and 'twitter' in the concluding lines of a slow-moving valedictory poem, serenely heavy with notions of departure and possibly death, is a *tour de force*. It prompts me to compare the close of 'To Autumn' with the elevated endings of two other, and even weightier, works in which serene acceptance is won after hard visionary experience. Both examples are from poets especially esteemed by Keats:

> His servants he with new acquist
> Of true experience from this great event
> With peace and consolation hath dismist
> And calm of mind all passion spent.
> (Milton, *Samson Agonistes*, 1755–8)

> Thanks to the human heart by which we live,
> Thanks to its tenderness, its joys, and fears,
> To me the meanest flower that blows can give
> Thoughts that do often lie too deep for tears.
> (Wordsworth, *Ode,*
> *Intimations of Immortality*, 201–4)

> Hedge-crickets sing, and now with treble soft
> The red-breast whistles from a garden-croft,
>   And gathering swallows twitter in the skies.
> (Keats, 'To Autumn', 31–3)

There remains the fragment, 'This living hand, now warm and capable', which was written on a sheet 'containing st. 51 of K's comic poem *The Cap and Bells*' (Allott, 700), and was probably composed in the last weeks of 1819. It may have been intended for a drama, because it is in blank verse, but nothing is certain about its provenance. It is haunting, and threatens an unknown person, possibly a potential murderer, with agonies of conscience if he does not take the hand. Wherever it belongs, it is fit to stand by itself without further comment.

> This living hand, now warm and capable
> Of earnest grasping, would, if it were cold
> And in the icy silence of the tomb,
> So haunt thy days and chill thy dreaming nights

> That thou wouldst wish thine own heart dry of blood
> So in my veins red life might stream again,
> And thou be conscience-calmed. See here it is –
> I hold it towards you.

In ending a chronological study of Keats's poems in this way, I have implied, in a way that I hope carries conviction, that there was, during the autumn of 1819, a development beyond what he achieved in the Spring Odes. After completing *Lamia*, and before the end of the year as far as is known, he had gone as far as he was to go in composing *The Fall of Hyperion*; he had revised and completed the ending of *Otho the Great* and made a strong start on *King Stephen*; he had written 'Bright star!' and 'This living hand'; and above all, he had composed 'To Autumn'. To my mind, these works exhibit a powerful visionary imagination expressing mature ideas and human feelings in forcefully concrete language, and, although the imagery is sparser than in his previous poems, it is if anything even more vividly moulded, and closer to the real subjects of the poetry.

Dominating those subjects, sometimes in direct confrontation and at other times by means of images which resist it, is the reality of death. This line of thought is established in earlier poems, with 'the sculptured dead' in their 'icy hoods and mails' in *The Eve of St Agnes*, and the 'death-pale' warriors of 'La Belle Dame Sans Merci'. It is there again in 'Ode to a Nightingale'. It proceeds further in the deaths of Lycius, in *Lamia*, and Ludolph, in *Otho the Great*. Lastly, there is the terrible fight against the 'palsied chill' of death in *The Fall of Hyperion*, when the poet struggles before the altar of Moneta, and manages to get his 'iced foot' on the lowest stair, which saves him. And in 'To Autumn' and 'This living hand' the reality of death is presented in a frame of harmonious acceptance and possible renewal.

10. The Forms of Keats's Poetry

Throughout his short career as a poet, Keats keenly deliberated questions of poetic form, considering each kind of line and stanza as it had been used by his predecessors and contemporaries, and developing his own practice in it according to his judgement and the proposed content. As often as not, he excelled previous practitioners in exploiting a form's possibilities and, towards the end, in the kinds of stanza he developed for his odes, he designed new ones. In his bare four years (1816–19) of poetic production, besides writing songs and other lyrics in various metres and stanza forms, he wrote in all the major forms of English poetry: Spenserian stanza, heroic couplet, *ottava rima*, octosyllabic couplet, blank verse and both kinds of sonnet, the Petrarchan and the Shakespearean. As will be shown, even his last three major poems, dating from the period July to September 1819, were each written in a different style and metre; and the differences are more marked than can be accounted for by their different genres – narrative in *Lamia*, lyric in 'To Autumn' and dream vision in *The Fall of Hyperion. A Dream*. The impression of constant experimentation is one reflection of Keats's frequent concern about his status as a poet, and of his healthy reluctance to feel self-satisfied about his achievement. Yet he did expect 'to be among the English poets' at his death. To understand his unwavering preoccupation with matters of poetic form is to go some way towards coming to terms with his achievement. The concentration on form in this chapter, with only incidental mention of language and content, suggests that it should be read in conjunction with the chapters where the poems being discussed receive their main comment.

Keats's first known poem, 'Imitation of Spenser', reflects his early enthusiasm for *The Faerie Queene*, and his sympathy with the still fashionable artistic preoccupation, originating in the late eighteenth-century, with the Middle Ages and early Renaissance. Keats followed eighteenth-century predecessors such as James Thomson in adopting, for his four-stanza poem, Spenser's verse form: a nine-line stanza, with eight lines of iambic pentameter and a concluding alexandrine, that is, a line with an extra foot, rhyming *ababbcbcc*. In its subject, a description of a lake island, and its language, which is lush and at times archaic, there are clear echoes of Spenser, Shakespeare, Milton and Thomson.

Most of the poems Keats wrote in the next two years are either occasional or on conventional subjects, such as sentimental romance and addresses to friends. Through them runs a thread that was to remain in his poetry until the end: his hope of becoming a major poet. Besides several stanza forms for songs and humorous poems, he mainly used these: the octosyllabic couplet, which in English poetry is usually light in effect and often satiric, the heroic couplet and the Petrarchan sonnet. He followed Leigh Hunt's example in breaking the formal structure of the eighteenth-century heroic couplet, which had been stigmatized by Southey, the fellow-poet of Wordsworth and Coleridge and Poet Laureate in Keats's day; thus: 'the detestable French heroic couplet, which epigrammatizes everything'. In its liberated form it early became Keats's standard metre for narrative, which he used not only for such long poems about poetry as *Sleep and Poetry* and 'I stood tip-toe upon a little hill' (both 1816) but also for his first and longest major poem, *Endymion* (1817). The 'breaking' of the couplet's formality was intended positively, to give a natural flow to intense poetic thought, couched in language not only freer and more sensuous than that of the eighteenth century but also less conventional, and less responsive to the generalizing impulse of received poetic diction.

Keats's chief prosodical means were: to abandon the regularity of end-stopped lines and the convention by which each couplet was a bounded unit of sense; to vary the position of the caesura; to permit frequent irregular stress; and to allow feminine rhymes more often than Dryden and Pope. Yet, although Keats's use of the heroic couplet was new, his language was at first still redolent of that of the eighteenth century, as such words as 'denizen', 'flowering bays' and 'morning sunbeams', in the next passage quoted, show. All the above characteristics appear in the extract, in which I have marked the main and minor stresses as well as the placing of the caesura:

> O Póesẙ// For thée I grásp my pén
> That ám not yét//a glórious dénizēn
> Of thy wíde héaven.// Yét, tō my árdent práyer,
> Yiéld from thy sánctuarẙ// some cléar aír,
> Smóothed for intóxicátion// bẙ the bréath
> Of flówering báys,// that Í may díe a déath
> Of lúxurẙ// and my yoúng spírit fóllow
> The mórning súnbeams// tō the gréat Apóllo
> Líke a frésh sácrifice . . .

> (*Sleep and Poetry*, 53–61)

In the major early poem in this metre, *Endymion*, almost half the 4,050 lines are run-on. Though the poem was begun only four months after 'I stood tip-toe upon a little hill', and was written at speed to a self-imposed timetable, *Endymion* reveals a marked, even sudden, development in Keats's power to present focused, condensed thought and strongly evocative images in language which is recognizably his own. Much of the poem is securely effective; a judgement which can be substantiated only by lengthy quotation. Here is the third stanza of the ode to Pan from Book I. Shelley noted 'its promise of ultimate excellence', but Wordsworth, after listening to Keats reciting it, sourly observed, 'A very pretty piece of paganism'. Keats's modest hope, which was expressed at the end of his preface to the poem, was: 'I hope I have not in too late a day touched the beautiful mythology of Greece, and dulled its brightness.' He need not have worried.

> 'Thou, to whom every faun and satyr flies
> For willing service, whether to surprise
> The squatted hare while in half-sleeping fit;
> Or upward ragged precipices flit
> To save poor lambkins from the eagle's maw;
> Or by mysterious enticement draw
> Bewildered shepherds to their path again;
> Or to tread breathless round the frothy main,
> And gather up all fancifullest shells
> For thee to tumble into naiads' cells,
> And being hidden, laugh at their out-peeping;
> Or to delight thee with fantastic leaping,
> The while they pelt each other on the crown
> With silvery oak-apples and fir-cones brown –
> By all the echoes that about thee ring,
> Hear us, O satyr king! . . .'

(263–78)

The puckish energy, the speed of ranging imagination, the natural vocabulary used unselfconsciously, are characteristic, and have their darker and more mysterious counterparts elsewhere in the poem, which, despite the difficulty of following every successive step in the hero's quests, and the occasional excesses and infelicities, repays every fresh reading.

After *Endymion*, during the writing of which he came to regard the influence of Leigh Hunt as detrimental to his own poetic art, Keats abandoned the heroic couplet for a while; and when he returned to it for the last time, in *Lamia* (1819), it is of a different kind altogether, and precisely harmonized to the sophistication of a new poetic vision (see pp. 144–5).

Of special interest is Keats's lifelong affair with the sonnet, which to begin with he worked fast and easily, often hurling thought into its strict form in a quarter of an hour. Although his few best sonnets are well known, it may surprise many to learn that two fifths of all his completed poems are in this form. The sonnet had had little special life in the poetic modes of the eighteenth century. Accordingly, the first Romantics, such as Wordsworth, drew strongly on Milton in their use of the Petrarchan sonnet, and on Shakespeare in their use of his form; in so doing, they aimed not to destroy a traditional form, but to use it to enrich their own poetry. The thirty-six sonnets Keats wrote up to the beginning of 1818 are all Petrarchan, following Milton and Wordsworth. This is the strict form, with an octave rhyming *abbaabba*, followed by a sestet of two tercets, rhyming either *cdcdcd* or *cdecde*. Keats observed its formality, which featured a statement of the main thought or problem in the octave, followed by the 'turn' (Italian: *volta*) to the consequent thought, resolution or refinement of the subject in the octave. Outstanding in this form is 'On First Looking into Chapman's Homer' (October 1816), the first of Keats's poems to be acknowledged by posterity as 'great'.

Most of the early sonnets express autobiographical matters and youthful enthusiasms, and Keats's improved accomplishment in the sonnet comes, significantly, with a move to the Shakespearean form. This is foreshadowed in the suddenly Shakespearean ending to the otherwise Petrarchan sonnet, 'On Sitting Down to Read King Lear Once Again' (January 1818). The next sonnet, written a day or two later, the well-known 'When I have fears that I may cease to be', which expresses Keats's perennial concern with love, death and his poetic destiny, is fully Shakespearean in form. Its lines are end-stopped, and its three quatrains are organically separate but logically successive. But the sense of the concluding couplet spills back into the twelfth line, thus making a fruitful link with the whole of the rest of the poem, and deliberately frustrating the epigrammatic tendency inherent in the regular form.

> . . . then on the shore
> Of the wide world I stand alone and think
> Till love and fame to nothingness do sink.
> (12–14)

That last feature of this fine poem becomes important in Keats's later thinking and practice in the sonnet.

Keats's subsequent sonnet-writing is spread over the last year and three quarters of his creative life, the twenty-six sonnets being predominantly in the Shakespearean form of three quatrains with alternate lines rhyming, followed by a concluding couplet. With the exception of 'When I have fears that I may cease to be', the six written in a burst, as Keats was starting on the composition of *Isabella; or, The Pot of Basil*, are light occasional poems.

For *Isabella*, his narrative poem based on a tale from Boccaccio's *Decameron*, Keats broke new personal ground in using *ottava rima*, the stanza of which consists of eight lines of iambic pentameter, the first six rhyming alternately, and the last two forming a couplet, *abababcc*. It is a form that Byron used in the same year for his mock-heroic *Beppo*. Since each stanza should be a unit, and the rhyming requirements are greater than those of the couplet, it is an exacting metre which forces strict discipline on the poet. Only occasionally does a poor rhyme distort the sense or lower the tone:

> . . . Those Baälites of pelf,
> Her brethren, noted the continual shower
> From her dead eyes, and many a curious elf,
> Among her kindred . . .
>
> (451–4)

But generally, whether the love-yearning of the heroine or the gruesome detail of the narrative is in process, the Gothic horror of the theme is expressed harmoniously, and the forceful description and imagery works well in the strict stanza form. Here is Isabella handling the rotting head of her murdered lover:

> In anxious secrecy they took it home,
> And then the prize was all for Isabel.
> She calmed its wild hair with a golden comb,
> And all around each eye's sepulchral cell
> Pointed each fringèd lash. The smearèd loam
> With tears, as chilly as a dripping well,
> She drenched away – and still she combed, and kept
> Sighing all day – and still she kissed, and wept.
>
> (401–8)

It may be useful to sum up the progress of Keats's craftsmanship at this point, which is often regarded, not least as it was by the poet himself, as the end of one stage of his poetic apprenticeship. He had decisively broken with the style of the eighteenth century, both metrically and in vocabulary, to achieve a new sort of fresh sensuousness and perception. After composing *Endymion*, he began better to control the exuberance which naturally fuelled his poetic practice, especially in the refinement of his vocabulary. He used a higher proportion of words of Anglo-Saxon origin, reduced the number of adjectives and adverbs, and developed stronger use of verbs. W. J. Bate (*The Stylistic Development of John Keats*, 1945, 31) notes in particular the steady reduction throughout Keats's career in the use of words of Latin origin: *Endymion* 15 per cent, *Isabella* 12.2 per cent, 'To Autumn' 8.3 per cent. Keats's placing of the caesura, and his patterns of stress and pause, began to be a little more regular. Most crucially, he recognized both the looseness and the monotony of the kind of rhymed couplet upon which he had relied in his three early long poems, *Sleep and Poetry*, 'I stood tip-toe upon a little hill' and *Endymion*. His resort in *Isabella* to *ottava rima* was the first result. The eight-line stanza worked as a paragraph, the disciplined use of which encouraged the development of shape and focus, with consequent intensity, in the treatment of a section of narrative or description.

It was Keats's ideal practice always to have a long poem on hand, but he never let that main process get in the way of his frequent urges to compose fast in a virtually extempore fashion on subjects of his immediate thought or experience. Thus, while he was working on *Hyperion*, he wrote a clutch of poems in a metre new to him: rhymed couplets in tetrameter with a dominant trochaic rhythm, of which lines 4 and 10 in the next quotation are good examples. These poems are light and exuberant, and the best known are the two related ones composed, most probably, soon after the death of Tom, in December 1818. They are 'Fancy' and the ode 'Bards of passion and of mirth', both of which are English Anacreontic odes. Anacreon was a Greek poet of the sixth century BC, who wrote lightly about love and drinking in simple stanzas of short lines. Keats sent them to his brother George and his sister-in-law Georgiana, describing them as 'specimens of a sort of rondeau'. The joyous mastery they exude typically celebrates poets and poetry; here the allegorized heroine of 'Fancy' is described at work:

> She will mix these pleasures up
> Like three fit wines in a cup,
> And thou shalt quaff it. Thou shalt hear
> Distant harvest-carols clear;
> Rustle of the reapèd corn;
> Sweet birds antheming the morn;

And in the same moment – hark!
Tis the early April lark,
Or the rooks with busy caw
Foraging for sticks and straw.

(37–46)

Hyperion (October 1818 to April 1819) and *The Fall of Hyperion. A Dream* (July to September 1819) are the only poems by Keats in blank verse, though of course his play *Otho the Great* and the dramatic fragment *King Stephen*, both of which date from the second half of 1819, were written in a broadly Shakespearean kind of blank verse. In the two poems the gain of writing in blank verse shows immediately in the absence of constriction by rhyme, and in freedom from embarrassment caused by poor or incongruous or forced rhyme. Besides this, blank verse offers better flexibility in the construction of poetic sentences, especially long sentences appropriate to narrative or to extended metaphor or similes.

The influence of Milton on the verse style of the first of these two poems is pervasive; Keats's marginal comments in his copy of *Paradise Lost* attest his profound reading and admiration of Milton, and to a reader who knows *Paradise Lost*, the first two books of *Hyperion*, especially, give off almost continuous Miltonic echoes. In the two short extracts which follow, there are long sentences, sustained by multiple clauses and run-on lines; epic similes; more Latinate language than in *Isabella*; deliberate repetition for effect; verbs, adjectives or nouns in threes for weighty effect; adjectives following their nouns instead of preceding them; past participles used as adjectives; adjectives used as adverbs following verbs; verbs used as nouns; inversion of the accent in the first foot of the line, usually with an accented verb; word music by planned variation of vowel sound, including assonance. Here are two passages from *Hyperion*, in which examples of these characteristics appear, with commentary: the first seven lines of the first passage contain an epic simile which describes the sound of the voice of Thea, wife of Hyperion, mourning with the fallen Saturn.

As when, upon a trancèd summer night,	*Every accented vowel a different sound* *Past participle as adjective*
Those green-robed senators of mighty wood,	*Past participle as adjective*

Tall oaks, branch-charmèd by the earnest stars,	*Past participle as adjective* *Assonance of three syllables*
Dream, and so dream all night without a stir,	*Repetition and assonance of two syllables* *Inversion of accent on first foot*
Save from one gradual solitary gust	*Inversion of accent on first foot*
Which comes upon the silence, and dies off	*Run-on line, paired assonance of 'upon' and 'off', 'silence' and 'dies'*
As if the ebbing air had but one wave;	*Every accented vowel a different sound*
So came these words and went, the while in tears	*Triple alliteration*
She touched her fair large forehead to the ground.	*Run-on line* *Every accented vowel a different sound*

(I, 72–80)

. . . Saturn must be king.

Yes, there must be a golden victory;	*Inversion of accent on first foot*
There must be Gods thrown down, and trumpets blown	*Repetition of verb, paired assonance ('must' 'trum', and 'thrown' 'blown')*
Of triumph calm, and hymns of festival	*Adjective following its noun* *Run-on line*
Upon the gold clouds metropolitan,	*Latinate adjective following its noun*
Voices of soft proclaim, and silver stir	*Two verbs as nouns, triple alliteration* *Inversion of accent on first foot*
Of strings in hollow shells; . . .	*Run-on line* *Alliteration continued from previous line*

(I, 125–31)

All good poetry is verbal music, and should be heard musically upon the ear. In his tribute to Milton, as in all his serious poetry, Keats

137

consciously aimed at a musical ideal, in which vowel sounds, and especially long and short vowels, 'should be interchanged, like differing notes in music'. Throughout her annotations in *The Poems of John Keats*, Allott notes echoes from other poets; but the echoes of, for example, Shakespeare and Wordsworth do not threaten the developing modes of Keats's poetic style in the same way that the conscious imitation of Milton does.

With *The Eve of St Agnes* (early 1819, revised in September), Keats moved towards his final and greatest technical achievement, the mastery of substantial stanza forms for narrative or lyrical purposes. The movement appears in this poem, in the last sonnets and above all in the Spring Odes of 1819. Keats had not used the Spenserian stanza, which he adopted for this poem, since writing his 'Imitation of Spenser'. The interlocking rhyme scheme of the stanza avoids the conclusive effect that Romantic poets disdained in the heroic couplet, an effect which also threatens in the final couplet of the *ottava rima* stanza, which Keats had used in *Isabella*, and in the final couplet of the Shakespearean sonnet. The longer last line of the Spenserian stanza, with the caesura in mid line, offers a slow lengthening for the rounding off and completion of a thought, a description or a narrated action. When handled according to its essential nature, the stanza is thus a harmonious poetic paragraph; and Keats, in following Spenser, strives for, and almost always achieves, the rhythm and unity of sense and adornment inherent in the form. Probably Keats adopted it because the material in his poem is located in a remote age of chivalry, not unlike that of *The Faerie Queene* except for the absence of allegory. Even allowing for the deliberate archaism of Spenser's style, Keats's technical mastery of the form, stanza by stanza, seems to me as good as, and often superior to, Spenser's.

Stanza xxiii of *The Eve of St Agnes*, in which Keats describes Madeline's arrival in her bedroom, full of dread anticipation of the spell to which she expects to subject herself, combines speed of concrete action and intensity of emotional experience in the kind of perfectly shaped nine-line paragraph which the Spenserian stanza offers. The action is in the first quatrain, and the fifth line makes a bridge of sense to the emotional interiority of the remaining lines, which is foreshadowed in the conclusion of the action quatrain. It is a regular stanza; all lines except the eighth are end-stopped, and the three inversions of accent on the line's first foot (lines 1, 6 and 7) all have strong rhetorical purpose. The many verbs give narrative strength to the stanza and its pervading emotion, and the profuse adjectives, which are more numerous throughout the poem than in either of the *Hyperion* poems, are all exact in sense. Even the apparently conventional 'balmy' reinforces the scented atmosphere of the poem as a whole, with Madeline's perfumed body at its centre. The nightingale image, so common in love poetry, is removed from epigrammatic banality by the run-on eighth line, and is turned upside down, into songlessness. It describes the agitated heart of Madeline as she struggles with the supernaturally imposed silence which is required if the spell is to work:

> Out went the taper as she hurried in;
> Its little smoke, in pallid moonshine, died.
> She closed the door, she panted, all akin
> To spirits of the air, and visions wide –
> No uttered syllable, or woe betide!
> But to her heart, her heart was voluble,
> Paining with eloquence her balmy side,
> As though a tongueless nightingale should swell
> Her throat in vain, and die, heart-stifled, in her dell.

The Spenserian stanza, it may be noted, was used by other Romantic poets. Keats was familiar with Byron's *Childe Harold's Pilgrimage*, the last canto of which had appeared in 1818. Byron became disillusioned with the poem's evidence of what he regarded as his youthful exaggerated romanticism, and for his epic satire *Don Juan* he turned to *ottava rima*, which I have already noted for its potential for general lightness, and for the epigrammatic facility in its concluding couplet, which Byron exploited with brilliant comic irony. Among the most distinguished uses by a Romantic poet of the Spenserian stanza was that of Shelley, in his gravely lyrical elegy on the death of Keats, *Adonais* (1821).

In *The Eve of St Mark* (February 1819), the short unfinished piece of medievalism which is generally regarded as a companion to *The Eve of St Agnes*, Keats returned briefly to the narrative couplet of four-stressed lines, mostly iambic but occasionally trochaic. It is evidence of, among other things, his continuous practical interest in the forms of poetry. This interest extended to the medieval ballad, a variant of which he developed in 'La Belle Dame Sans Merci' (April 1819). This variant, the stanza comprising three four-stressed iambic lines and a concluding shorter line, rhyming *xaxa*, had been used by Coleridge (in 'Love', 1799) among others; and, typically, Keats infused the form with his own imprint, making the last line of each stanza slow and heavy, the stressed syllables being scantily supported by unstressed ones. Indeed, those last lines could reasonably be scanned as two-stressed, rather than the three of Coleridge:

> And the harvest's done
> Fast withereth too
> And made sweet moan
> On the cold hill side

The effect they create is one of something like a ghostly refrain, running right through the poem.

In this last year of constant production, the several different forms in Keats's poetry were developed in a rush, virtually together. There are the short poems in various metres, of which 'La Belle Dame Sans Merci' was only one; the sonnets span the period; *Lamia*, written in a new kind of heroic couplet, overlapped with *The Fall of Hyperion. A Dream*; and the odes culminate in September with the profound lyric 'To Autumn'.

In the spring of 1819 Keats returned to the sonnet after a pause of at least five months – a long period in view of his often casual use of it for occasional light-hearted effusions. His last previous sonnet, written in August 1818 on the summit of Ben Nevis, had been, like all the sonnets worth serious attention that he was to write from now on, in some sort of Shakespearean form. I write 'some sort' because of the variety of irregularities he practised with the aim of finding the ideal form. Among the irregularities are: failure to observe the division between the octave and the sestet, or the placing of the *volta* nearer to the end than the eighth line; ignoring the quatrain structure of Shakespeare, especially in the octave; and varying the rhyme scheme in the sestet in several ways, chiefly to avoid the hammer blow of a detached final couplet.

Thus we find, besides the regular *efefgg* rhyme scheme in the sestet, *efeggf* ('How fevered is the man who cannot look'), and *bcefef* ('To Sleep'). In the most haunting of all his sonnets, 'As Hermes once' (April 1819), Keats runs together the two quatrains of the octave, and turns on the *volta* with the antithetical word 'but'. His last sonnet, 'Bright star!' (late 1819), has the regular Shakespearean rhyme scheme, but its structure is Petrarchan, having one long verse sentence as octave, a powerful *volta* in the single word 'No', and a fully continuous sestet, though there is an almost separate closing couplet. His search for the ideal form is expressed in his letter to George and Georgiana of 3 May 1819: 'I have been endeavouring to discover a better sonnet stanza than we have. The legitimate [by which Keats means the Petrarchan] does not suit the language over-well from the pouncing rhymes [Keats is acknowledging the scarcity of rhyme sounds in English, in contrast to their plenty in French and Italian] – the other kind [by which Keats means the Shakespearean] appears too elegiac – and the couplet at the end of it has seldom a pleasing effect – I do not pretend to have succeeded.'

In fact, Keats begins the last of his experimental sonnets, which is about this problem, with 'If by dull rhymes our English must be chained'. He had at least once followed his own implied advice by writing an unrhymed sonnet, 'O thou whose face hath felt the Winter's wind' (February 1818). Others had experimented with rhymelessness: in 1801 Southey had written a long poem, *Thalaba the Destroyer*, in unrhymed but otherwise complex stanzas of mixed long and short lines. Keats searched for a stanza 'more interwoven and complete' (line 5 of 'If by dull rhymes'); and of course he had already found and successfully used one, the Spenserian. In it he had mastered the problem of rhyme, but as he had conformed with precedent in using that stanza only for narrative, he needed a new long 'interwoven and complete' stanza for other purposes. This he was to develop, with ever more fruitful variation, in the Spring Odes of 1819.

These Spring Odes emerge as a sequence of meditation on the subject of most importance to Keats, one which had found intermittent expression in much of the poetry he had already composed: the beauty and the permanence of art, the comparative ephemerality of life and joy, and the ideal of love, which in such a setting is necessarily melancholic. The realization of this vision, which Keats aimed at and achieved, involved the presentation and meditative analysis of revealing linked images, not a narrative unfolding such as he had achieved in *Hyperion*. So his resort in form was not to the Spenserian stanza, but rather to the sonnet, which is ode-like on a small scale, and usually presents a single but detailed and often complex image in a seriously lyrical mode. The process by which Keats created an 'interwoven and complete' stanza without the formal disabilities of either kind of sonnet shows clearly in the Spring Odes, each of which has the length of a short sonnet sequence. 'Ode to a Nightingale', the longest, would have been a sequence of six sonnets. 'Ode to Psyche' has four verse paragraphs of different lengths, respectively of twenty-three, twelve, fourteen and eighteen lines. It is therefore an English version of the Pindaric ode, which in Greece had a complex metrical structure with varying lengths of line and stanza reflecting dance and song patterns. In fact, in each stanza of 'Psyche' the structure of the sonnet is drawn upon. The opening vision of the poem, of Psyche and Cupid making love in a forest, begins with a sonnet, the octave of which is Shakespearean, and the sestet of which is slightly irregular Petrarchan (*cdecce*), with the twelfth line, suddenly, a trimeter: 'A brooklet, scarce espied'. Each verse paragraph has three or four such lines, the sense effect of which is climactic because they interrupt the prevailing pentameter pattern to which the hearing mind is accustomed, while their musical effect is to achieve fluidity and excitement, and to dispose of any echoes of regular forms such as sonnet, heroic couplet or Spenserian stanza. Their climactic effect is used to complete the joyful hope with which the poem ends: 'To let the warm Love in!' An indication of Keats's fastidiousness concerning rhyme is that, uniquely in the Spring Odes, four lines in the poem, 10, 15, 44 and 45, are left unrhymed presumably because any rhyme-words which suggested themselves would have harmed the sense.

Evidently the irregular form of 'Ode to Psyche' was one that Keats thought he would not repeat, because the next three odes, 'Ode to a Nightingale', 'Ode on Melancholy' and 'Ode on Indolence', are stricter in form. The measure is a Shakespearean quatrain followed by a Petrarchan sestet (*cdecde*), with this notable difference, that in 'Ode to a Nightingale' the fruitful trimeter occurs in every stanza, in the eighth line. After 'Ode to a Nightingale' (assuming 'Ode on Indolence' to have been composed last of the group – see p. 67), Keats drops the short line altogether, and the resultant ten-line stanza of regular iambic pentameter becomes a firm verse paragraph, always dealing with a defined part of the subject from its beginning to its close. It is erroneous to think of each such stanza as a kind of mini-sonnet, because the thought of a sonnet is complete in itself, whereas in the Spring Odes, the rounding-off thought at the end of a stanza leads forward to further development, like the end of a good prose paragraph. The increased regularity of form here outlined is repeated in the regularity in the lines themselves, which are mostly unbroken, while there are fewer of the run-on lines which Keats had written deliberately, and with almost doctrinaire justification, at an earlier stage of his career. In addition, inversion of the accent becomes rarer and, as earlier, occurs mostly on the first foot of the line.

In harmony with these prosodic changes, the language changes too. There are more short words, and fewer words of Latin origin; and there is more reliance on strong consonantal clusters. The musical arrangement of sounds is still continuously addressed, and the assonantal and alliterative patterns mentioned in the discussion of *Hyperion* remain common. Thus, in the opening of the 'Ode on Melancholy' there are two lines containing two assonantal pairs:

> By nightshade, ruby grape of Proserpine

> Nor let the beetle, nor the death-moth be

The last stanza of 'Ode on a Grecian Urn', with its three broken lines (1, 4 and 9), its heavy slowness (lines such as 46, 'When old age shall this generation waste'), and its subtle alliteration on 'm' (lines 2 and 7–8) and 'n' (line 10), nicely demonstrates how, after proceeding for a time with musical regularity, a poet may achieve a final effect of solemn conviction: all but one of the ten stressed syllables in the last two lines contain long vowels.

'To Autumn', which stands apart from the Spring Odes of 1819 in subject and spirit, as well as having been composed four months later, takes musical regularity to perhaps its ultimate point in the scheme of Keats's practice in prosody. First of all, he adds a line to the ten-line stanza of the Spring Odes, and makes a couplet before the final line, so that the whole stanza of eleven-line regular iambic pentameter rhymes *ababcdedcce*. By the way Keats treats it, the 'couplet' belies its name, for the material in it is bound grammatically to what precedes and follows it:

> And sometimes like a gleaner thou dost keep
> Steady thy laden head across a brook;
> Or by a cyder-press, with patient look,
>   Thou watchest the last oozings hours by hours.
>   (19–22)

The effect of the prosodic innovation is to give a rounded power to the rhythm of each stanza-statement in the poem, the whole of which is unassailably tranquil. The first stanza is all direct maturing plenitude; the second personifies Autumn at work in that plenitude; and the third is an evocation of the air and sky above the autumnal scene, in which sounds of birds and insects predominate, making a kind of sung elegy for the end of harvest. The language is amazingly simple, coming from a poet who, in August 1820, just before leaving for Italy fatally ill, was to advise Shelley 'to load every rift with ore'. It is more monosyllabic and Saxon than most of what he wrote, and so full of long vowels and clusters of consonants that, reading it, one is forced to go slowly, and take account of a general spondaic effect, even though true spondees are rare. Thus, from the opening stanza, phrases such as 'close bosom friend', 'mossed cottage-trees', 'with a sweet kernel' and 'until they think warm days' encourage a meditative slowness of utterance. One line, 'While barrèd clouds bloom the soft-dying day', does this heavily, with great weight on the first half of what is an irregular line. The characteristic has been observed in the last lines of each stanza of 'La Belle Dame Sans Merci'.

The gravely beautiful lyricism and regularity of 'To Autumn' is paralleled in narrative mode in Keats's last two narrative poems to be considered here, on which he seems to have been working simultaneously up to September 1819. To take *The Fall of Hyperion. A Dream* first. Since Keats's purpose in writing the poem was to reconstruct the abandoned *Hyperion*, yet to include some passages from the earlier poem, there was no question that the metre would be anything but blank verse. But as the new poem was conceived as a dream vision, in which the poet's striving for immortality entitles him to hear from Moneta of the fall of the Titans, the verse, and particularly that of the new introduction (1–293), is subtly different from the blank verse of *Hyperion*. The interiority of the poet's struggle and the suffering of Moneta are expressed personally, in an intimate and even dream-like way different from epic narration. The passages from the earlier poem which remain seem to me to stand out curiously in the new creation, just as a few lines from *The Fall of Hyperion. A Dream*, which Keats included in *Hyperion* when preparing it for publication, strike the characteristic later note. *The Fall of Hyperion. A Dream* is less Miltonic than *Hyperion*, although Keats was still to abandon it, as he had abandoned *Hyperion*, because he considered the style to be too artfully Miltonic. There are fewer inversions, and in the reworking of passages from *Hyperion*, minor archaisms, such as 'eterne' and 'couchant' are removed as Keats aims at a more natural diction. Perhaps it was the filtering of classical material through the consciousness of the struggling poet which made Keats's friends prefer the earlier poem: critical disagreement about the relative merits of the two poems still exists.

The process of purifying his poetic diction and use of form went at the same time, in another narrative poem, in a surprising direction; to the emulation of Dryden, with whose works he had long been admiringly familiar. Some time during the summer of 1819 Keats studied Dryden's language and narrative method in rendering into heroic couplets two tales from Boccaccio, *Sigismonda and Guiscardo* and *Cymon and Iphigenia*. As a result, he produced *Lamia*. As with his use of metres established by other poets – Spenser, Shakespeare, Milton – Keats aimed not to imitate, but to take the best features and adapt and transcend them in fulfilment of his own poetic purposes. In returning to the metre which, in *Endymion*, composed two years before, he had stretched and deformed in defiance of eighteenth-century practice, Keats was to perfect his control of the orthodox form, whatever effect this might have on the originality of poetic expression that he had demonstrated so far. In *Lamia* end-stopped lines and enclosed couplets feature commonly with assurance and grace, and the caesura is mostly placed in a regular position, after the second or third foot of the line. One feature is Keats's frequent use of the alexandrine, a legitimate resort when composing in heroic couplets: almost all the thirty-eight such lines mark a full close to the grammatical sense unit, as if Keats felt some nostalgia for the function of such lines in the Spenserian stanza. Another permitted variation is the triplet, of which there are eight examples in Book I, while the whole poem ends resoundingly with a triplet which includes an alexandrine:

> On the high couch he lay – his friends came round –
> Supported him – no pulse, or breath they found,
> And, in its marriage robe, the heavy body wound.

The weight of the language is less than in the Spring Odes; diphthongs, long vowels and consonantal clusters are rarer, so that narrative speed is gathered. In addition, conscious assonantal patterning is sparse, as in *The Fall of Hyperion. A Dream*. Generalizing and conventional adjectives are often preferred to inspirational Keatsian ones, as in this passage describing the effect of wine and music on the guests at Lamia's wedding:

> Soft went the music the soft air along,
> While fluent Greek a vowelled undersong
> Kept up among the guests, discoursing low
> At first, for scarcely was the wine at flow;
> But when the happy vintage touched their brains,
> Louder they talk, and louder come the strains
> Of powerful instruments. The gorgeous dyes,
> The space, the splendour of the draperies,
> The roof of awful richness, nectarous cheer,
> Beautiful slaves, and Lamia's self, appear,
> Now, when the wine has done its rosy deed,
> And every soul from human trammels freed,
> No more so strange . . .
>
> (II, 199–211)

Besides the first line, only 'vowelled undersong' in all that description has for me the touch of the inspired Keats, and characteristically it is his sense of the music in speech that prompts the phrase. But 'happy vintage', 'awful richness', 'nectarous cheer' and 'has done its rosy deed' seem to me to resurrect a generalizing kind of poetic diction characteristic of the English Neo-Classical style. Indeed, Woodhouse pronounced the poem to be 'Drydenian heroic', which referred to the diction and metre rather than to the subject. Keats achieves the composed and graceful swing of Dryden, but, in doing so, he sometimes renders less vividly than the subject deserves the brilliant sensuous perceptions which are the essence of the poem before its chill conclusion.

These mild strictures should not be pushed too far. Richness does play its part in the language pattern of the poem, and at times such early Keatsian characteristics as the compound adjective contribute to it. The well-known first description of Lamia herself, before her transformation into a beautiful human girl, contains such epithets as 'vermilion-spotted' and 'rainbow-sided', and the immediately preceding account of Hermes approaching her bombards the reader with four examples such as might have been found in *Endymion*:

> The God, dove-footed, glided silently
> Round bush and tree, soft-brushing in his speed
> The taller grasses and full-flowering weed,
> Until he found a palpitating snake,
> Bright, and cirque-couchant in a dusky brake.
>
> (I, 42–6)

The continuous ambiguity of Keats's attitude to his subject seems to be reflected in the uncertain variety of the language, and in the alternation between sensuous commitment and half-disgusted detachment. After all, the charms of Lamia are shown to be delusive, and there is something relentless about the exposure by Apollonius of his disciple's spook paramour; there may be a limit to the linguistic decoration which should be accorded to hard truth.

Whatever judgement may be made about *Lamia*, it appears to me certain that *The Cap and Bells; or, The Jealousies*, the satiric 'fairy tale' in Spenserian stanzas which Keats wrote next, shows a decline in Keats's powers and, more especially, in his poetic judgement. The choice and mode of subject may have been determined by a wish to emulate Byron's comic satirical achievement in *Don Juan*, Cantos I and II of which had appeared in July 1819. But the mode aimed at, which offers amused criticism of its subject as from a distance, resists the Keatsian principle of intensity, and it is kinder to the poet to account for the existence of this supposedly cheerful and witty, but more often facetious, poem, on pragmatic, external grounds. His health was failing; his brother George was on the way back from America broke and in search of money; and, above all, the impossibility of his being able to marry Fanny completed a darkening scene. With his friend Brown he therefore looked for light relief in busily working at a humorous poem. After *The Cap and Bells*, he wrote, as far as we know, only one or two heart-breaking lyrics addressed to Fanny, for whom his love, as he struggled against coming death, was now out of control.

But the last of these poems, which Keats dignified with the title 'Ode to Fanny', interestingly features a new kind of stanza. It is an eight-line stanza, rhyming *abaccbdd*, with four regular lines of iambic penta-meter, 1–3 and 6. The intervening and closing rhyming couplets are of various lengths, the concluding couplet being in every stanza but the first, trimeters. Even in such an obsessive poem as this, Keats is explor-ing the possibilities allowed by the form of the ode. The last stanza expresses the jealousy which disfigured his mind as he slid into despair:

> Ah, if you prize my subdued soul above
>   The poor, the fading, brief pride of an hour,
> Let none profane my Holy See of love,
>   Or with a rude hand break
>   The sacramental cake;
> Let none else touch the just new-budded flower.
>   If not – may my eyes close,
>   Love, on their last repose.

Select Bibliography and Abbreviations Used in the Text

	Abbreviation
ALLOTT, M. *The Poems of John Keats*, 1970	Allott
BARNARD, J. *John Keats: The Complete Poems*, 1976	
—*John Keats*, 1987	Barnard
BATE, W. J. *John Keats*, 1964	
—*The Stylistic Development of John Keats*, 1945	
BATE, W. J. (ed.) *Keats: A Collection of Critical Essays*, 1964	
BUTLER, M. *Romantics, Rebels and Reactionaries*, 1981	Butler
FRASER, G. S. (ed.) *Odes: A Selection of Critical Essays*, 1975, 1981	Fraser
GITTINGS, R. *John Keats*, 1968	Gittings
—*John Keats, the Living Year*, 1954	LY
GITTINGS, R. (ed.) *The Letters of John Keats: A Selection*	Letters
HILL, J. S. (ed.) *The Narrative Poems: A Casebook*, 1983	Hill
JACK, I. *Keats and the Mirror of Art*, 1967	
JONES, J. *John Keats's Dream of Truth*, 1969	
LEMPRIÈRE, J. *Classical Dictionary*, 1788, 3rd edition, 1987	Lemprière
MATHEWS, G. M. (ed.) *Keats: The Critical Heritage*, 1971	
RICKS, C. *Keats and Embarrassment*, 1974	
ROLLINS, H. E. *The Keats Circle*, 1948	
ROLLINS, H. E. (ed.) *The Letters of John Keats, 1814–1821*, 1958	
WARD, A. *John Keats: The Making of a Poet*, 1966	Ward
WILSON, K. M. *The Nightingale and the Hawk: A Psychological Study of Keats's Ode*, 1964	

Literary Glossary

Abbey, Richard (176?–1837). Sole guardian of the Keats children after his fellow-guardian Sandall fled to Holland. Was mean in administration of their inheritance, was against Keats being a poet, and tried to keep Fanny away from her brothers. p. 1

Bailey, Benjamin (1791–1853). Friendly with Keats from spring 1817 to 1819. Keats stayed with him in Oxford while composing part of *Endymion*. pp. 2, 13

Blake, William (1757–1827). Visionary poet and engraver; member of the 'first' generation of Romantic poets. Like Keats, a Londoner. Had a profoundly revolutionary view of Christianity and government, which he expressed in his Prophetic Books, in his collections of aphorisms such as *The Marriage of Heaven and Hell* (*c.* 1790–93), and in his lyrics such as *Songs of Innocence* (1789) and *Songs of Experience* (1795). pp. 8, 26, 62

Boccaccio, Giovanni (1313–75). Poet on whose works Chaucer based *The Knight's Tale* and *Troilus and Criseyde*; prose writer of the *Decameron* (*c.* 1349–51), Keats's source for *Isabella*. pp. 30–32, 134, 144

Brawne, Fanny (1800–1865). Probably met Keats soon after his return from Scotland. Lived next door from October 1819 till May 1820. With her mother, nursed Keats during August and September 1820 till his departure for Italy. pp. 2, 3, 15, 33, 54, 64, 67, 118–22, 147

Bridges, Robert (1844–1930). Poet Laureate from 1913. Editor and critic of Keats's poems. pp. 21, 72

Brown, Charles Armitage (1787–1842). Inherited a fortune and so was able to be a gentleman of letters. Friend and patron of Keats from summer 1817. Went with Keats to Scotland in 1818, and took Keats into his home after the death of Tom. Travelled with Keats in 1819 to the Isle of Wight and Winchester. Collaborated with him on *Otho the Great*. After Keats's death quarrelled with Taylor, Reynolds, Dilke and George Keats. pp. 2, 11, 113–14, 121

Burns, Robert (1759–96). Scotland's chief poet, and collector and writer of Scottish songs, who was profoundly admired by English Romantic poets. When Keats came to the Burns country on his Scottish tour, 'he felt a self-identification with Burns' (Gittings, 333) on account of his poetic achievement and political stance, his lowly origins and early death. p. 29

Burton, Robert (1577–1640). Author of *The Anatomy of Melancholy*, 1621, 'a storehouse of anecdote and maxim' upon melancholy, 'an inbred malady in every one of us' (*Oxford Companion to English Literature*, 1985, 26b). The source of Keats's *Lamia*. pp. 61, 64, 68, 91, 100–101

Byron, George Gordon, Lord (1788–1824). Member, with Shelley and Keats, of the 'second generation' of Romantic poets. Prolific writer of poems, plays and journals. Best-known works: *Childe Harold* (Cantos I and II, 1812; III, 1816; IV, 1818) and *Don Juan* (1819–24). In poetic taste, an anti-Romantic at heart, who preferred Pope and Dryden and their successors to the Lake Poets, and especially to Keats. pp. 1, 3, 8, 10, 16, 18, 26, 34, 74, 106, 113, 123, 134, 139, 146

Cary, Henry Francis (1772–1844). Translator of Dante's *Divina Commedia*. His blank verse translations of the *Inferno* (1805), and the *Purgatorio* and *Paradiso* (1814), were known and admired by Keats, who took them as his sole reading on his Scottish journey with Brown in 1818. pp. 1, 2, 35

Chapman, George (1559?–1634). Prolific contemporary of Shakespeare who wrote many successful plays and translated Homer. See Keats's sonnet 'On First Looking into Chapman's Homer'. pp. 17, 133

Chatterton, Thomas (1752–70). Wrote pseudo-archaic prose and poetry, the medieval provenance of which he tried to establish with forged documents. He failed to further his career by these means, and committed suicide at the age of eighteen. However, he deceived the Romantic poets into accepting him posthumously as a heroic genius rejected by his fellow-men, and Keats dedicated *Endymion* to him. pp. 27, 52

Clarke, Charles Cowden (1787–1877). Son of the headmaster of Keats's school. Friend of Keats at school, and till 1817. Author, publisher and lecturer. pp. 5, 9–10

Coleridge, Samuel Taylor (1772–1834). Member of the 'first generation' of Romantic poets. With Wordsworth, wrote *The Lyrical Ballads* (1798). Besides being known best as a poet, he was a Christian polemicist, journalist, philosopher and literary critic. Keats knew his work well and met him in 1819. pp. 2, 8, 12, 26–7, 56–7, 67, 72, 76, 113, 131, 139

Colvin, Sir Sidney (1845–1927). Critic who wrote a life of Keats (1887). p. 118

Dante Alighieri (1265–1321). Poet of the *Vita Nuova* (1290–94) and the *Divina Commedia* (1307?–21), and writer in both Italian and Latin of philosophical and literary treatises. Greatly influenced many English poets, including Chaucer, Milton and especially the Romantic poets. Shelley and Byron greatly admired him, and in Keats's mind he gradually became much more important than Milton. Later he greatly influenced T. S. Eliot. pp. 1, 2, 12–13, 35, 60–61, 102, 108

Dryden, John (1631–1700). Prolific poet, dramatist, translator and polemicist of the Restoration period. Upon hints from Hazlitt, who preferred Dryden to Pope, Keats studied his work intensively in 1819, an interest reflected in *Lamia*. pp. 12, 27, 30–31, 131, 144–6

Empson, Sir William (1906–84). Poet and critic, author of *Seven Types of Ambiguity* (1930) and *The Structure of Complex Words* (1951). pp. 84–5

Godwin, William (1756–1836). At first a Dissenting minister, who became an atheist. Author of *Enquiry Concerning Political Justice* (1793), in which his theory of human perfectibility, which Keats expressly supported, was developed. Radical politician and novelist, husband and supporter of Mary Wollstonecraft, author of *A Vindication of the Rights of Woman* (1792) and mother of Mary Shelley. p. 2

Graves, Robert von Ranke (1895–1985). Poet, novelist, translator, critic. Author of *The White Goddess: A Historical Grammar of Poetic Myth* (1948). pp. 64, 69

Haydon, Benjamin Robert (1786–1846). Unsuccessful painter of huge canvases on historical and classical subjects. Met Keats at Leigh Hunt's in October 1816. Befriended him, encouraged him in writing poetry, introduced him to the Elgin Marbles, and borrowed money from him. Pioneer theorist on art education and industrial design. His journals contain vivid accounts of his literary and other friends, including Keats. pp. 2, 16

Hazlitt, William (1778–1830). Essayist and critic. Was attacked by *Blackwood's* for being associated with the 'Cockney' school of poetry. The most important single influence on Keats, especially with his *Lectures on the English Poets*, 1818, and his firm liberal stance in politics. His ideas often appear in Keats's letters and poetry. pp. 2, 13–14, 40, 99

Homer. Thought to be the first and greatest poet of the ancient Greeks, and author of the *Iliad* and the *Odyssey*. Modern scholarship questions these assumptions. See under 'Chapman' above. p. 17

Hunt, James Henry Leigh (1784–1859). Poet, essayist and editor of the *Examiner*, the first publication to include any of Keats's work. Edited the *Indicator* 1819–21. Supporter of the Romantic poets, especially Shelley, Keats and, later, Byron. By reason of his literary journalism and his poem *The Story of Rimini* (1816), he was regarded as the central figure in the so-called 'Cockney' school of poetry. pp. 1, 2, 3, 7, 11, 16, 18, 60, 99, 131–2

Lamb, Charles (1775–1834). Essayist, friend of Wordsworth and Coleridge and the younger Romantics. p. 32

Lemprière, John (d. 1824). Author of *Bibliotheca Classica* (*Classical Dictionary*), 1788, Keats's main source for mythological and historical matter concerning the classical world of Greece and Rome. pp. 6–7, 17, 57

Milton, John (1608–74). Poet whose *Paradise Lost* (1667) is the best-known epic in English. Milton was also a polemicist on behalf of the Commonwealth, to whose Council of State he was Latin secretary (1649–60). His reformist writing on religious, political, social and educational matters, including 'The Doctrine and Discipline of Divorce' (1643) and 'Areopagitica' (1644), in which he defended the liberty of the press, influenced the Romantic poets almost as much as his poetry, but for Keats his poetic influence, which shows most strongly in *Hyperion*, was paramount. pp. 12–13, 16, 27, 35–6, 39, 41–2, 67, 70, 72, 87, 90, 92, 102–3, 108–10, 128, 130, 133, 136–7, 144

Ovid (Publius Ovidius Naso) (43 BC–AD 18). Latin poet of the Augustan Age, whose *Metamorphoses*, a collection of mythological stories in verse, has been mined by English poets, including Chaucer, Shakespeare and Keats. p. 24

Petrarch *see under* 'Petrarch' in *Literary Terms*. p. 155

Pope, Alexander (1688–1744). Poet, translator and satirist of the English Augustan Age, who stood for the Neo-Classical values in poetry which Keats resisted. Favoured by Byron above contemporary Romantic poets. pp. 9, 17, 27, 30, 131

Reynolds, John Hamilton (1796–1852). Fellow-poet of the youthful Keats, who met him in October 1816 and exchanged many letters with him. pp. 2, 11–12, 29–30, 103

Selincourt, Ernest de (1870–1943). Professor of Poetry at Oxford, 1928–33, and specialist in the Romantic period. p. 118

Severn, Joseph (1793–1879). Engraver, then painter. Friend and supporter of Keats. Accompanied Keats to Italy when Brown did not reply to Keats's request, and looked after the poet until he died. pp. 2, 16

Shakespeare, William (1564–1616). Ever present in Keats's mind. References to, and quotations from, his work abound in the poems and letters. pp. 11–12, 13, 16, 23, 30, 37, 45–6, 48, 56, 59, 63, 67, 72, 75–6, 112, 114–16, 118–9, 122, 130, 133–4, 136, 138, 140, 144

Shelley, Percy Bysshe (1792–1822). Fellow-poet of Keats, with whom he was in touch from 1817 (during the composition of *Endymion*) till Keats's death. In 1820 invited Keats to stay with him in Italy, where he had settled in 1818. pp. 2, 3, 8, 10–11, 17, 20–21, 26, 34–6, 56, 113, 132, 139

Southey, Robert (1774–1843). Poet and critic, lifelong friend of Coleridge. Poet Laureate from 1813. Attacked Byron, in whose *The Vision of Judgement* and *Don Juan* Southey is often the butt of hilarious mockery. pp. 27, 131, 141

Spenser, Edmund (*c*. 1552–99). Major Elizabethan poet and author of *The Faerie Queene* (1590 and 1596). The first poet who seriously influenced Keats, with both the metre and the medieval-style subject of his great poem. pp. 1, 12, 16, 44, 63, 130, 138, 141, 144–5

Taylor, John (d. 1864) and **Hessey, James Augustus** (d. 1870). Publishers who took over Keats's *Poems 1817* from the Ollier brothers and, convinced of his greatness, lent him books and money despite hostile reviews. pp. 2, 11, 22, 50, 97

Thomson, James (1700–1748). Scottish poet and dramatist who moved to London in 1725 and was, of all eighteenth-century poets, the one most esteemed by the Romantic poets. This was on account of his writing about nature in *The Seasons* (1726–30), which inspired some of the paintings of J. M. W. Turner and supplied the libretto for Haydn's oratorio *The Seasons*. p. 130

Virgil (Publius Vergilius Maro) (70–19 BC). Chief poet of the Roman civilization. His epic poem, the *Aeneid*, celebrates Rome from its origins to its becoming an empire. pp. 1, 5

Woodhouse, Richard (1788–1834). Legal adviser to Taylor & Hessey, who collected and copied everything he could of Keats's writing. Severn described him as 'the active and discriminating friend of Keats . . . to whom we owe the preservation of his finest productions'. pp. 2, 11, 14, 28, 32, 67, 145

Wordsworth, William (1770–1850). Member of the 'first generation' of Romantic poets, and generally regarded as the leading poet among the Romantics. Became Poet Laureate on the death of Southey (1843). Joint author, with Coleridge, of the *Lyrical Ballads* (1798), which is still regarded as heralding the new age of Romantic poetry. He began as a liberal supporter of the French Revolution, but became a conservative establishment figure, to the dismay of the 'second generation' of Romantic poets. 'Byron and Shelley mocked him as "simple" and "dull", Keats distrusted what he called the "egotistical sublime", and Hazlitt and later Browning, deplored him as "The Lost Leader", who had abandoned his earlier radical faith'

153

(*Oxford Companion to English Literature*, 1085b). Keats praised *The Excursion* (1814). pp. 1, 8, 12–14, 16, 18, 26–7, 29, 72, 106, 113, 128, 131–3, 138

Glossary of Literary Terms

alexandrine	a twelve-syllable iambic line
anacoluthon	ungrammatical sequence in sentence construction
Anacreon(tic)	a Greek lyric poet of the sixth century BC who wrote light poems about love and conviviality in short lines
assonance	imperfect rhyme, usually of vowel sounds but not consonants, as in *take* and *mate*, or of consonants but not vowel sounds, as in *craft* and *croft*
blank verse	unrhymed iambic pentameter
caesura	a slight pause in a line of poetry, usually between phrases, e.g.

> Then to my human heart/I turn at once.

Cavalier	describes poets generally on the Royalist side during the English Civil War in the mid seventeenth century; their lyrics tended to be urbane and witty
end-stopped	describes a line of poetry which ends with a strong pause in the sense but not necessarily with a full stop
epic simile	a simile extended through several lines, sustaining a comparison in a style appropriate to epic poetry
feminine ending	an extra unstressed syllable at the end of a line of verse, e.g.

> Thy fáted hóur. That thóu hadst pówer to dó so

feminine rhyme (or double rhyme)	The rhyming of two or more lines with feminine endings, e.g.

> Fancy – high commissioned send her!
> She has vassals to attend her.

heroic couplet	a rhymed pair of lines in iambic pentameter, which in the regular form is always end-stopped. Keats varied this
iamb(ic)	a poetic foot of two syllables, the second of which is stressed
octave	the first eight lines of a sonnet
ode	a lyric in lofty style, usually addressed formally to its subject. Originally, in ancient Greece, it was sung (see **Pindar**)

Critical Studies: The Poetry of Keats

ottava rima	a stanza of eight lines of iambic pentameter, rhyming *abababcc*
pentameter	a line of five metrical feet
Petrarch(an)	(1304–74) Italian poet who gave his name to the form of the sonnet followed in English by Milton and the early Keats. It consisted of an octave of eight lines, in two quatrains, rhyming *abbaabba*, and, after a structural pause, a sestet of six lines, in two tercets, rhyming *cdecde* or *cdcdcd*
Pindar(ic)	(*c.* 522–443 BC) Greek lyric poet whose name is used to distinguish the kind of lofty and formal ode consisting of stanzas of various forms, including a triadic structure and irregular rhyme schemes. In English, developed first by Abraham Cowley (1618–67)
quatrain	a unit of poetry of four metrical lines
sestet	a unit of poetry of six metrical lines
Shakespearean sonnet	sonnet consisting of four quatrains and a final couplet, rhyming *ababcdcdefefgg*
Spenserian stanza	the stanza invented by Edmund Spenser (*c.* 1552–99), in which he wrote *The Faerie Queene*. It consists of nine lines of iambic pentameter, the last of which is an alexandrine (see above), rhyming *ababbcbcc*
spondee (spondaic)	a metrical foot of two stressed syllables, e.g. And no bírds síng
tercet	a poetic unit of three lines
tetrameter	a poetic line of four metrical feet
trimeter	a poetic line of three metrical feet
trochee (trochaic)	a metrical foot of two syllables, the first of which is stressed
volta (Italian 'turn')	the change in thought and feeling which in the sonnet, and especially the Petrarchan, signals the end of the octave and the beginning of the sestet

Index to Keats's Poems

Italicized page numbers refer to the main discussion of the poem cited.

Addressed to Haydon ['Great spirits now on earth are sojourning'], 16
'As Hermes once took to his feathers light', 3, 13, 58, *60–62*, 64, 92, 140

'Bright star! Would I were steadfast as thou art', 112, *121–2*, 129

Calidore. A Fragment, 16
Cap and Bells, The, 3, 44, 112, *122–3*, 128, 146

Endymion: A Poetic Romance, 2, 6, 7, 10, 11, 15, 16, *20–28*, 29, 56, 57, 67, 90, 103, 106, 113, 131, 132, 135, 144, 146
Eve of St Agnes, The, 3, 10, 16, *44–51*, 52, 54, 57, 97, 118, 124, 129, *138–9*
Eve of St Mark, The, 3, 44, *51–3*, 54, 123, 139

Fall of Hyperion. A Dream, The, 3, 6, 7, 11–13, 21, 27, 43, 62, *102–11*, 112, 119, 122, 124, 129–30, 136, 144–5
'Fame, like a wayward girl, will still be coy', 60
Fancy, *54–8*, 103, 135

'How fevered is the man who cannot look', 60
'Hush, hush! Tread softly! Hush, hush, my dear!', 44
Hyperion. A Fragment, 3, 6–8, 12, 28–30, *34–43*, 54, 59, 102–3, 108–9, 124, 135–6, 141–2, 144

'I cry your mercy, pity, love', 120
'I stood tip-toe upon a little hill', 10, 17, *19–20*, 131
'If by dull rhymes our English must be chained', 141
Imitation of Spenser, 130
'In drear-nighted December', 20
Isabella; or, The Pot of Basil, 2, 3, 10, 29, *30–33*, 44, 82, 118, *134*, 135–6

King Stephen, 3, 112, *117–18*, 119, 129, 136

La Belle Dame Sans Merci, 3, 58, 60, *62–4*, 66, 90, 92–3, 118, 129, *139–40*, 143
Lamia, 3, 10, 13–14, *90–101*, 112, 117, 129–30, 133, 140, *144–6*

'O Solitude, if I must with thee dwell', 2
'O thou whose face hath felt the Winter's wind', 141
Ode ['Bards of passion and of mirth'], *54–5*, 67, 135
Ode on a Grecian Urn, 3, 6, 66, 68, 72, *79–85*, 143
Ode on Indolence, 3, 11, 66–8, *88–9*, 142
Ode on Melancholy, 3, 68, *85–8*, 142
Ode to Apollo, 67
Ode to Fanny, 67, *120–21*, 147
Ode to May. Fragment, 67
Ode to a Nightingale, 3, 66, 68, 72–9, 85, 120, *141–2*
Ode to Psyche, 3, 6, 66, 68, *69–72*, 103, *141–2*
On First Looking into Chapman's Homer, 2, 17
On Sitting Down to Read *King Lear* Once Again, 30
Otho the Great, 3, *112–17*, 119, 129, 136
'Over the hill and over the dale', 29

Sleep and Poetry, 2, 10, 17–19, 59, 102, 131, 135
Song about Myself, A, 29
Song of Four Fairies, 66

'The day is gone, and all its sweets are gone!', 119
'This living hand, now warm and capable', *128–9*
To Autumn, 3, 67, 90, 101, 112, 119, *124–9*, 130, 140, *143–4*
To — [Fanny], 119–20
To J. H. Reynolds, Esq., 29, 30, 83, 88
To Sleep, 60, 66, 140

'When I have fears that I may cease to be', 133
'Where be ye going, you Devon maid?', 29
'Why did I laugh tonight? No voice will tell', *58–9*, 76, 88
'Woman! When I behold thee flippant, vain', 17
Written in Disgust of Vulgar Superstition, 17
Written on the Day that Mr Leigh Hunt left Prison, 17

The Letters of John Keats, 4, 7, 8, 12, 13, 14, 15, 20, 22, 26, 30, 32, 33, 55, 58, 61, 69, 84, 87, 89, 90, 97, 99, 103, 125, 140–41

Discover more about our forthcoming books through Penguin's FREE newspaper...

Penguin
Quarterly

It's packed with:

- exciting features
- author interviews
- previews & reviews
- books from your favourite films & TV series
- exclusive competitions & much, much more...

Write off for your free copy today to:
Dept JC
Penguin Books Ltd
FREEPOST
West Drayton
Middlesex
UB7 0BR
NO STAMP REQUIRED

FOR THE BEST IN PAPERBACKS, LOOK FOR THE 🐧

In every corner of the world, on every subject under the sun, Penguin represents quality and variety – the very best in publishing today.

For complete information about books available from Penguin – including Puffins, Penguin Classics and Arkana – and how to order them, write to us at the appropriate address below. Please note that for copyright reasons the selection of books varies from country to country.

In the United Kingdom: Please write to *Dept JC, Penguin Books Ltd, FREEPOST, West Drayton, Middlesex, UB7 0BR*.

If you have any difficulty in obtaining a title, please send your order with the correct money, plus ten per cent for postage and packaging, to *PO Box No 11, West Drayton, Middlesex*

In the United States: Please write to *Dept BA, Penguin, 299 Murray Hill Parkway, East Rutherford, New Jersey 07073*

In Canada: Please write to *Penguin Books Canada Ltd, 2801 John Street, Markham, Ontario L3R 1B4*

In Australia: Please write to the *Marketing Department, Penguin Books Australia Ltd, P.O. Box 257, Ringwood, Victoria 3134*

In New Zealand: Please write to the *Marketing Department, Penguin Books (NZ) Ltd, Private Bag, Takapuna, Auckland 9*

In India: Please write to *Penguin Overseas Ltd, 706 Eros Apartments, 56 Nehru Place, New Delhi, 110019*

In the Netherlands: Please write to *Penguin Books Netherlands B.V., Postbus 3507, NL–1001 AH, Amsterdam*

In West Germany: Please write to *Penguin Books Ltd, Friedrichstrasse 10–12, D–6000 Frankfurt/Main 1*

In Spain: Please write to *Alhambra Longman S.A., Fernandez de la Hoz 9, E–28010 Madrid*

In Italy: Please write to *Penguin Italia s.r.l., Via Como 4, I-20096 Pioltello (Milano)*

In France: Please write to *Penguin France S.A., 17 rue Lejeune, F-31000 Toulouse*

In Japan: Please write to *Longman Penguin Japan Co Ltd, Yamaguchi Building, 2–12–9 Kanda Jimbocho, Chiyoda-Ku, Tokyo 101*